Transforming Students

Transforming Students

Fulfilling the Promise of Higher Education

CHARITY JOHANSSON and PETER FELTEN

Johns Hopkins University Press

Baltimore

© 2014 Johns Hopkins University Press
All rights reserved. Published 2014
Printed in the United States of America on acid-free paper

2 4 6 8 9 7 5 3 1

Johns Hopkins University Press
2715 North Charles Street
Baltimore, Maryland 21218-4363
www.press.jhu.edu

Library of Congress Cataloging-in-Publication Data

Johansson, Charity.
Transforming students : fulfilling the promise of higher education /
Charity Johansson and Peter Felten.
     pages cm
     Includes bibliographical references and index.
     ISBN-13: 978-1-4214-1437-9 (pbk.) ISBN-10: 1-4214-1437-6 (paperback)
     ISBN-13: 978-1-4214-1438-6 (electronic)
     1. Transformative learning. 2. Higher education—Aims and
objectives. 3. College students—Attitudes. 4. Elon University—
History. I. Felten, Peter. II. Title.
     LC1100.J64 2014
     370.11'5—dc23   2013043571

A catalog record for this book is available from the British Library.

*Special discounts are available for bulk purchases of this book. For more
information, please contact Special Sales at 410-516-6936 or
specialsales@press.jhu.edu.*

Johns Hopkins University Press uses environmentally friendly book
materials, including recycled text paper that is composed of at least
30 percent post-consumer waste, whenever possible.

CONTENTS

Students inspired this book. We are grateful to every student who we interviewed, who recommended a friend to us, or who taught us along the way.

We also are grateful to all the faculty, staff, alumni, and parents who shared their stories and perspectives with us. In particular, we are grateful to the assistance of Mary Knight-McKenna, Katie King, and Jean Eckrich for helping with the interviews, asking us hard questions, and sharing their expertise. Desiree Porter and Laura St. Cyr assisted with the index. We also thank Ed Wilson and Patricia Johansson for their thoughtful reviews of the manuscript.

Megan Scribner provided essential editorial assistance throughout the writing process. With her challenge and support, we transformed hundreds of pages of interview transcripts into a book.

The concept for the book was conceived while Charity served as the faculty fellow and special assistant to the president at Elon University. President Leo Lambert has provided both the freedom and the support necessary to bring this work to fruition.

And finally, we wish to thank our families whose love and encouragement have sustained us through many long nights and short weekends as this book unfolded.

Transforming Students

We live in transformational times. Colleges and universities are struggling to adapt to a radically new environment. The economic crisis has devastated budgets just as demands for accountability and outcomes continue to increase. Student demographics are shifting, redefining the characteristics of a typical undergraduate. Emerging technologies are challenging long-held assumptions about where, how, and when faculty teach, why students need to live together on a campus, and what it means to learn.

To confront these and other challenges, we should resist solutions offered by the technology du jour and focus on the fundamental purposes of higher education. As Wendell Berry (1987) reminds us, "The thing being made in a university is humanity. . . . Underlying the idea of a university—the bringing together, the combining into one, of all of the disciplines—is the idea that good work and good citizenship are the inevitable by-products of the making of a good—that is, a fully developed—human being" (77). If we take Berry's message seriously, we should concentrate our efforts on the mission of undergraduate education. We need to return to the work of transforming students.

When we write of transformation, we are *not* suggesting that higher education should mold students into a specified form, belief system, or mind-set. Colleges do not make widgets. But colleges can play an important role in cultivating transformation understood as an ongoing process of intentionally aligning one's actions and behaviors with one's evolving sense of identity. Such learning and development, of course, can happen in many places and at many points during life, not just in college. Transformation is the work of a lifetime, not simply a task to pursue over four ivy-covered years. What higher education can do, what we must do, is prepare students for a life of continuing change and development. Our purpose is to help students both transform themselves and understand the process of transformation so that they are well-equipped to embrace change and flourish after they graduate.

The undergraduate years are a unique opportunity for transformation. Many students enter college at a ripe developmental moment, yearning to understand themselves and to connect with something bigger. Higher education cannot guarantee that this degree of change will take place, but we can provide curricular and cocurricular experiences that challenge students' current views, guide them in the examination of their assumptions, and offer them the chance to construct an emerging sense of self and relationship with the world. An engaging undergraduate education gives students multiple opportunities to act on their own values and test their commitments in complex situations. In this way, college is like a practice room where a musician hones her craft, struggling and failing to hit all the notes until finally, after diligent work and with guidance from mentors, she is ready to perform on the stage.

While the practice room is an appealing metaphor, it raises a fundamental question: What exactly does higher education prepare students to do? What are undergraduates practicing for? These days, some call for a more vocational orientation that would generate graduates who are ready for particular workplaces or careers. The need for practical skills and knowledge is powerful, but a narrow attention to specific and existing jobs ignores the reality of the rapidly changing world our graduates will enter. Economic commentators frequently remark on the number of jobs that college graduates are likely to hold over their careers, often in fields that haven't yet been invented. And employers are seeking out people with broad capacities to meet these changing demands. A 2013 report by Hart Research Associates, for example, notes that college graduates' "demonstrated capacity to think critically, communicate clearly, and solve complex problems is *more important* than their undergraduate major" in hiring decisions (emphasis in original).

Rather than solely or even primarily preparing graduates for particular jobs, higher education must prepare students to navigate our complex and rapidly evolving world. While we cannot possibly know everything they might face in the future, we do know the general sorts of things our students will encounter. They will live and work with diverse peoples and cultures, requiring them to understand and cooperate across differences. The economy and workplace will continually change, prompting them to assess often incomplete information and adjust nimbly. Their values and beliefs will be confronted, leading them to weigh competing commitments.

The particulars of these and other future challenges are impossible to see clearly. The only way to prepare for these anticipated unknowns is to practice being reflective, resilient, and innovative. We can create opportunities for students to develop these qualities by prompting them to approach important problems with an open and inquisitive mind, to learn to have civil discourse before being faced with a crisis, and to reflect critically on values before being forced to choose in a dynamic environment. In our classrooms and dormitories, in the lab or in off-campus and online experiences, we must provide that practice for students.

By engaging in a learning process that is not merely informative but transformative, students have the opportunity to practice these life skills thoughtfully and consciously. While they are arriving at new understandings, they are also becoming aware of the process of transformation itself, thus being positioned to recognize and welcome opportunities for development later in their lives. This prepares them for lifelong learning and to think purposefully about *what* they should do and *why* they should do it. Learning that is transformative is characterized by a deep and enduring change in thinking that is evidenced through changed ways of being in the world.

This shift can appear epochal, seemingly a result of an epiphany or dramatic event, but it is typically a more extended and cumulative process. Though not strictly linear in its progression, transformative learning tends to follow four general steps: (1) beginning with a *disruption* of a previous way of looking at the world, (2) followed by *reflective analysis* of one's underlying assumptions, (3) *verifying* and *acting on* these new understandings, and, finally, (4) *integrating* these new ways of being into everyday life. The chapters of this book roughly follow these phases.

- Chapter 1 explores the complex nature of "home" in the college environment. On the threshold of change, students live in the tensions between a safe and comfortable environment and a place from which to venture out into new territory.

- In chapter 2, we examine how disruptions of the student's beliefs and assumptions create openings for deeper learning. This is essential but tricky work, balancing challenge and support in dynamic situations.
- How students reflect in order to learn and develop is the focus of chapter 3. Knowing how to actively engage in both internal and external dialogues is an important skill that students must cultivate to effectively analyze their assumptions and contexts.
- For learning to be transformative, new perspectives and commitments must be acted upon. In this process of verification, the subject of chapter 4, students work to take action in ways that are consistent with who they want to become.
- Chapter 5 explores the important role relationships play throughout the transformative learning process and how colleges can foster relationships to facilitate deep and ongoing learning.
- Finally, in chapter 6, we look at the transformative process at the institutional level, because students' experiences of deep and lasting changes are most likely to take place within the context of organizations that are themselves engaged in the same process.

Throughout this book, we synthesize research on learning and development in higher education. The literature on transformative learning is rooted in the field of adult education (Mezirow and Taylor 2009; Taylor and Cranton 2012); we apply those tenets here to emerging adults (Arnett 2004), traditional college-age students attending residential colleges. These same principles are undoubtedly relevant to other settings—older students, nonresidential settings, online learning, and so on—but our book is aimed at the particularly rich and promising opportunity of residential colleges to facilitate transformation among young adults.

This book explores this process by listening carefully to the students, faculty, staff, alumni, and parents at one institution. Elon University is a private university in North Carolina with about 5,300 undergraduates who come from across the country and around the world. Most Elon students live on the 620-acre campus, and all share a common liberal arts and science core curriculum, supplemented by nationally accredited professional and graduate programs. Campus life is characterized by engaged learning that takes place in close partnerships with faculty and staff. Encouraging students to integrate learning across the disciplines and to put knowledge into practice, the university endeavors to prepare students to be global citizens and informed leaders motivated by a concern for the common good.

In our research approach, we were inspired by Loren Pope's *Colleges That Change Lives* (Pope 2000; Pope and Oswald 2012) and Richard Light's *Making the Most of College* (2004). Pope notes that one characteristic of deep and significant change is that the person whose life is changed wants to tell his or her story. Light spent more than a decade asking his Harvard students to reflect for him on their college experiences. With those models in mind, we went in search of stories of transformation. We interviewed scores of students, along with faculty, staff, and alumni, in search of personal stories that clarify the nature of transformative learning and make accessible the findings of existing research and literature from multiple fields. We have included their names with their permission.

Although this story is told primarily from the perspective of individuals affiliated with one institution, we do not claim that Elon is uniquely successful in reaching its transformational goals. These stories exist, in some variation, at every college; they are local and personal yet also universal. By drawing on stories from a single institution, we have minimized the need to explain the context of each narrative. The power is in the stories themselves, not in the institution. To add clarity and contrast to our analysis, we periodically provide examples from other schools and from higher education scholars. We believe these examples and personal stories illustrate and illuminate the larger themes of effecting change in ways that resonate with faculty, staff, administrators, students, and parents. We hope that this narrative approach equips our readers with the means to make the transformative potential of college more intentional and powerful.

There is no recipe for something as serendipitous as transformation. We cannot guarantee that kind of change with any student, but we do believe (and research suggests) that certain practices can increase the potential in an individual and an environment. All of the people who touch the lives of undergraduates—faculty, staff, and administrators on campuses, but also parents, coaches, mentors, and friends, and, of course, the students themselves—can contribute to that potential.

When undergraduate education aims to be transformative, the benefits accrue to more than just the individual students themselves. The more that attention to transformation is woven into the institution—the more students are taking enlightened action within the college community, the more faculty and staff aspire toward student transformation—the richer the college environment becomes. Students inspire their peers with their own experiences, insights, and courage. Colleagues encourage each other to bring out the best in their students. Structures and practices at the institution support openness, reflection, and change. In a setting like this, students themselves come to embody, and even enlarge, the university's mission of transformation.

This is the essence of the book: transformational learning changes people for a lifetime. The goal of the transformative learning process in college is that students emerge with a powerful combination of knowledge, skills, and commitment; that they see the work that needs to be done, the contributions that need to be made, the things in the world that need to be changed; that they have the capacities and the confidence needed to contribute to those changes; and that they have a sense of both agency and urgency.

The same goals apply to this book. We hope you will come away from it seeing the value of transformative learning, believing in your power to affect that process, and having the skills to facilitate it. Only when we do these things are we fulfilling the promise of higher education for our students, our institutions, and our world.

CHAPTER ONE

On the Threshold

As a high school senior in Virginia, Bre Detwiler applied to fourteen colleges. After being admitted to thirteen, Bre and her father "got in the car and drove down and drove up and drove over." She found her college home in Elon, North Carolina: "We loved Elon. There was something so safe about it."

Bre was not referring to Elon as a "safety school" that she would attend if her more ambitious plans did not work out. Nor was she referring to physical safety, although she and her father shared some concern about her habit of going for late evening runs.

Instead, Bre—and many of the other students we interviewed—used words like "safe" to describe their immediate sense of comfort with the campus. Eric Brown recalls that he narrowed his college choices to two and then, after visiting both, "I decided that Elon had a much more familiar feeling to it." Myra Garcia visited all six of the colleges that admitted her, but "I just didn't find the same feeling that I felt at Elon. . . . It felt so friendly and welcoming." Sarah Gould describes her experience on a campus tour as a more passionate one: "It was just one of those situations where I got to Elon and I absolutely fell in love with it. I don't know what it was, but I just walked away with a sense of, 'That's the type of place I want to be.'" Jill Medhus speaks for many of her peers when she concludes, "When I stepped onto Elon's campus, it really felt like home."

Leaving (and Finding) Home

The sentiments of these Elon students could be those of many undergraduates across the country. Colleges and universities strive to nurture a sense of belonging, of "home" in their students. And for good reason. Vincent Tinto's (2012) influential research on college student retention emphasizes the importance of students' feeling welcomed and valued on campus. The initial challenge for a college, then, is for its students to feel immediately at home in a place they've never lived before.

Residential colleges like Elon do this intentionally by crafting admissions materials and first-year experiences that invite the students to feel a part of the institution (Greenfield, Keup, and Gardner 2013). They design beautiful campuses, organize orientation sessions, establish students in homelike dormitory rooms, and foster community interactions. During their first semester at Elon, for instance, all students take Elon 101, a one-credit seminar course that supports their transition into the academic community with class experiences designed to enhance students' academic and interpersonal skills, to encourage social responsibility and personal integrity, to foster respect for individual differences, and to model a passion for lifelong learning.

Concordia University in St. Paul, Minnesota, also offers a one-credit first semester seminar for all its students. The Concordia seminar centers on questions about student engagement and mentorship, although the topical focus varies. At Concordia, students select a seminar based on topic, while Elon students are placed in the seminar based primarily on scheduling needs. In both cases, as in the many other such courses at other universities, a core goal of these first-year seminars is to orient students into their new academic community (Greenfield, Keup, and Gardner 2013, 110–11).

But stories of students finding a new "home" on campus demonstrate more than just the significance of the actions of faculty teaching first-year seminars and resident advisors in the dorms. The incoming students' desire for a safe haven at this point in their lives also plays a role. Tim Clydesdale (2007) goes so far as to conclude that most first-year college students are "largely immune to intellectual curiosity and creative engagement" (153). Rather than exploring big questions and seeking worthy dreams, Clydesdale argues, most first-year students create an "identity lockbox into which [they] can place their critical religious, political, racial, gender, and class identities for safekeeping [as undergraduates]" (39). The world is too wobbly and unstable for these students to do more than cling to the familiar while they focus their energy and time on daily life management. Clydesdale's depiction of the average college student's need to remain intellectually and emotionally "indoors" does not create much space for the transformation that colleges aim to facilitate in their students.

Jeffrey Arnett's theory of "emerging adulthood" (2004) also emphasizes instability and "feeling in-between" as distinguishing features of life on the threshold of college. Arnett, however, concludes that this uncertainty, rather than locking these students in, primes them for identity exploration, marking college as an age of possibilities. Emerging adults, he claims, actively try on diverse identities before donning the more enduring characteristics they will maintain through later years. They consider several possible selves (Markus and Nirius 1986), playing out both the hopes and fears of who they might become. From this perspective, students seek college as a home base for their wide-ranging explorations, not a place to hide out.

Although our interviews uncovered sentiment that fits the extremes of both Clydesdale's and Arnett's analyses, the stories we heard revealed that most students have more nuanced attitudes about what they want out of college. Students are seeking *both* a comfortable, familiar place that feels like home *and* a safe base from which to venture out to try new things, confident that they have a secure place to recover from and reflect on their explorations. In this way, our interviews reflect recent scholarship that emphasizes the fluidity and intersectionality of student identity (Torres, Jones, and Renn 2009). College students, like other people, do not have a single, fixed identity; as Lisa Bowleg explains, there may be many times "when Black + lesbian + woman ≠ Black lesbian woman" (2008). A student will identify as a male athlete in one context, an aspiring physician in another, and as a hip hop fan in a third. Throughout college, students are exploring the intersections of various parts of their emerging identities, often struggling with perceived conflicts between different aspects of the same self.

We see this tension in students' desires when they first step onto campus. While they hope to feel safe and at home, they don't want to actually *be* at home. And though they may identify themselves as "seekers" who are questioning fundamentals and looking for deeper meaning, they tend to affiliate with peers who look and act and think much like themselves (Chickering, Dalton, and Stamm 2006; Evans et al. 2010). They expect to change; they even want to change, just not too much. They know they are entering a liminal space in college, although few would call it that. They are in-between and simultaneously welcome and shy away from what is coming. They know that a college campus is a transitional home for them, a space between their childhood and adult lives, and their feelings about this are complex and evolving. As 24-year-old Jedediah Purdy (quoted in Parks 2011, 46) wrote, "We doubt the possibility of being at home in the world, yet we desire that home above all else."

Becoming More of Who I Am

This paradoxical view seems to express itself in a vision of change shared by many entering college students. In our interviews, we found that most students come to college expecting to evolve, but they believe they will become more of the person they already are, not someone new. They do not expect to change in any fundamental way, nor do they anticipate being transformed. For instance, Olivia Hubert-Allen explains, "Initially, I didn't anticipate I would change much. I felt like I already had a pretty solid foundation of who I was. . . . I wanted to be more of myself. " Ben Smith, too, echoes these sentiments: "When I came into college, I thought that I was pretty set in the way that I was . . . and I didn't think I had that much potential to change. At 18, you think you're right about everything, and I didn't think I had that much left to learn. I don't think I expected to change this much."

This common first-year student expectation to evolve but not be transformed is not altogether unrealistic; not all change is transformational. In college, young people are making choices that will affect their futures. "What's my major going to be?" "Who should I room with next year?" "Should I go Greek?" "Where will I study abroad?" These are certainly potentially formative decisions but not necessarily *trans*formative. For transformation to occur, change must be deep and lasting, touching close to a core identity. But much of what students experience in college (and what we, in general, experience in our lives) just rubs at the margins of our identities, leading to new preferences and transient changes in our thinking or behavior, if it affects us at all.

Even when students do expect to change in college, they rarely anticipate big changes, and they certainly don't expect the upheaval that often accompanies those deeper changes. As she prepared to enter her first year at Elon, Zana Milak, for example, predicted that the most difficult challenge she would face in college would be picking an academic major. "I think deciding what I really want to go into, what I really want to do, is going to be the hardest part about college." Students like Zana may anticipate occasional rough sailing during college, choppy waters they must navigate, but rarely do they anticipate intense difficulties that might cause them to reframe their understanding of themselves. That's not surprising. Ruthellen Josselson, a leading identity scholar, notes: "Living our identities is much like breathing. We don't have to ask ourselves each morning who we are. We simply are." (1996, 29)

Models of student development, such as those of William Perry (1998) and Marcia Baxter Magolda (2001), highlight important and common transitions in students' experiences as they move through college. This development is rarely linear or steady; few individual students progress predictably through some theoretical sequence. Instead, students' identities are in flux while they find their way in complex social networks, shifting back and forth as they adapt to new contexts. As Josselson posits, students—and all people—embody "both change and continuity" simultaneously (1996, 29), what Robert Kegan calls "dynamic stability" (1982).

Despite the apparent churning in some students' lives, on a day-to-day basis the alterations tend to be small and additive. Students learn to write more clearly and to solve more complex math problems. They become more adept at leading peer groups and at navigating diverse social settings. They eat new food, connect with different people, and take up new habits, hobbies, and areas of study. They may even get tattooed. Despite the cumulative weight of these small steps, taken together these rarely do more than scratch the surface of a student's sense of his or her own identity. Without significant challenges, students rarely change in more than superficial ways.

Crossing the Threshold

When students first arrive on campus, they carry backpacks heavy with habits, beliefs, expectations, and relationships that will shape their experiences in college. Some of these enable students to experience exciting growth and change. Others constrain, leading them to be cautious about or even fearful of what's ahead. Whatever the nature and balance of the things they are carrying, all first-year students, whether they realize it or not, stand on the threshold of transformation. They are poised to begin to question, to experiment, to change. To fulfill the promise of undergraduate education, colleges and universities need to help students become aware of the liminal nature of their position, to become competent if not comfortable, while balancing in the space between their former and future selves.

For all of us who work with and mentor students at colleges and universities, our role is to support them in holding these diverse selves in tension, allowing new depths of meaning to emerge. Given the inherently molten developmental state of most college students, higher education institutions should seek to create deliberate opportunities for growth. Unlike the students, colleges should anticipate and encourage more than mere additive change. We should seek to foster deeper, transformative changes.

We believe college faculty and staff have a key role in assisting students toward meaningful, lasting learning and development. We are not limited to designing curricula and programs to foster academic transformation. We also often guide students individually and in groups through the maze of life during college. As Clydesdale reminds us, first-year students often are unable or unprepared to transition from focusing on daily life management to noticing the big changes that are possible for them. They need scaffolding as they construct and reconstruct their identities. Colleges are positioned to provide that support, complementing the infrastructure many students already have from their parents and families, their faith communities, and other groups beyond campus.

Students can and do transform without explicit prompting, but focused attention from the moment students step onto campus makes it more likely that students' changes will occur in intentional and positive ways. Well-chosen encounters can facilitate openness to such deep and meaningful change during the college years. They can stimulate curiosity and instill courage, encouraging students to stretch themselves. These experiences often emerge from disruptive activities or thought-provoking ideas designed by faculty and staff to challenge students to go beyond their comfort zones.

For instance, the Michigan Community Scholars Program (MCSP) at the University of Michigan demonstrates the potential of including intentional challenges and disruptions from the start of the undergraduate experience. The curricular and cocurricular MCSP programs focus on questions of diversity. Each year, some 125 first-year students are selected to join this residential learning community so that the group represents the racial, ethnic, and international makeup of the university. Not only do MCSP students study diversity, they also wrestle with its implications in their day-to-day interactions in their learning community. While this program may make many students uncomfortable at times, the impressive academic and student development outcomes of MCSP demonstrate the value of this direct approach to immersing at least some first-year undergraduates in an environment ripe for disruption (Greenfield, Keup, and Gardner 2013, 134–35).

Ironically, the yearning for a sense of home that often draws students to a particular college may be at odds with a desire for this kind of challenge. Sarah Gould's comment illustrates this point: "I don't think I came to Elon with the intent of changing. Part of the reason why I liked Elon was because when I was on campus, it did feel very similar to home." Larissa Ferretti, who said she was "really comfortable" with herself when she came to college, elaborates on this idea: "I came to college thinking I really knew who I was, but when I got here—I think there are a few months when you're kind of in shock and you feel like, 'Oh my goodness, I don't really know who I am, and I still have a lot more to explore!' I think I still don't really know exactly who I am. I'm becoming okay with that I guess, and becoming okay with the idea that it's a constant learning process. . . . I definitely didn't expect the transformation that happened."

So while we initially strive to make our students feel comfortable on campus, we then must help them balance their desire for security with the need to take risks and explore new ideas and possibilities. Rather than attempting to resolve the tension, a college should help students find their place on this precarious threshold, in the liminal space between the familiar and strange, the old and the new. As Sharon Parks reminds us, "It is a responsibility and privilege to participate in the process by which others become at home in the universe" (2011, 49).

Disruption, Reflection, Verification

Transformative learning has been the subject of considerable scholarship over the past forty years (e.g., Mezirow and Taylor 2009; Taylor and Cranton 2012), but its roots have been firmly planted in the field of adult education.

By casting our focus on the emerging adult, the traditional college-age student, we can shed light on the separate steps in the transformational learning process, steps which college faculty and staff are in a unique position to facilitate.

Though not strictly linear in its progression, transformative learning tends to move through somewhat predictable stages, which we outlined in the introduction and review here. These steps may be familiar to those of us who work with undergraduates, even if we have never studied theories of student or adult development. The process begins with the disruption of a previous way of looking at the world, typically an uncomfortable experience the student may not willingly or eagerly move into. A student might enroll in a course without realizing that some of her fundamental assumptions are going to be destabilized, or a student might select a roommate without realizing the ways living side-by-side with someone can raise unexpected questions about life choices. This disorienting process calls into question the learners' prevailing views about themselves or the world, priming them to challenge the assumptions that have previously supported that view.

Then reflective analysis—employing critical thinking, dialogue, and intuitive discernment to examine their assumptions—opens the learner to other possible ways of seeing the world around them and their place in it. During this stage, learners have the opportunity to experiment with different perspectives and to thoughtfully select the view that most closely aligns with what they believe—or perhaps to change a long-held belief to reflect a new understanding they have developed. This identity exploration, according to Arnett and others, is a natural and necessary component of maturation. When this exploration draws on well-examined values and assumptions, the emergent choices tend to be deeper and more persistent.

In order to ensure lasting change, learners must then act on these new choices and test their new outlook against their ongoing experiences. This process of verification allows learners to refine their views, reinforce the importance of the change, and build their confidence and skill in acting on these values. Finally, for full integration, this way of being must be woven into the fabric of ordinary life. Everyday decisions and behaviors must sustain the transformation.

Each of these phases contains distinct elements. For example, the "initial disruption process," which we explore in the next chapter, involves readiness, exposure, engagement, and investment. The "reflective analysis" phase tends to involve critical analysis of assumptions as well as individual discernment and shared dialogue with others. "Verification" typically includes steps linked to making decisions, taking action, and developing skills and confidence. Finally, as learners engage in practices that sustain these attitudes and behaviors, this new way of viewing and responding to the world becomes an integral part of who they are.

The intentional effort to foster student transformation does *not* imply that colleges should try to transform students into something specific. Even at a college with a particular mission, such as developing students in the context of a specific religious tradition, individuals need the freedom to grow in their own ways and at their own pace. The transformative learning process should help students build an identity rooted in their own sense of purpose and meaning in the world, but it is not a uniform path walked by all. As students make their own way, we should support and challenge them to reach toward their potential, changing and developing who they are in ways that are radical—deeply rooted—and also true to their evolving sense of identity. Our goal should be to help.

CHAPTER TWO

Creating Openness

"I can't do this anymore!" sobbed Amy Rittenour over the phone to her mother. "I'm dropping out of the Honors program." The experience that brought Amy to this crisis point was a course during her third semester of college entitled "Exploring Consciousness," team taught by professors in psychology and religious studies. "It just kind of blew everything that I had ever thought about myself and religion, and the world and spirituality, and all this other stuff out of the water," Amy recalled in our interview, "I had to start from scratch."

"Just give it a chance," her mother said. "I know it's hard."

Amy's mother was right. "And you know," Amy later told us, "it was really difficult. Probably only within the past one and a half years or so have I really been able to come to understand and appreciate what they did, because honestly, I was very frustrated even at the end of that semester. It made me totally rethink what I had been taught for the past however many years and what I wanted to think for myself rather than what people were telling me. Those experiences that really make you totally reexamine where you've been coming from for the past nineteen years of your life are some of the hardest moments. But that ended up being a really, really beneficial thing."

College faculty and staff know that new experiences are important for student learning and development; a student's reach should exceed her grasp. We design courses, programs, and activities that expose students to greater levels of challenge, previously unknown aspects of the world, and different life perspectives. We do this believing that causing some disequilibrium opens the way for change that we hope will be significant and lasting—indeed, transformative. But we also know that we cannot know which students will be affected by a particular set of experiences. The results of our efforts can seem frustratingly random and unpredictable. In this way, our aspirations for student transformation also should exceed our grasp. We need to till the soil to create the best possible environment for seeds of change to sprout, even though we recognize that no one course or program can guarantee growth.

Despite the difficulty of the task before us, we should intentionally and carefully help move students beyond the eagerness and excitement of new experiences into, as Amy can attest, discomfort and frustration, into the trying experience of disorientation. Of necessity, students in this state will find themselves on a fault line, a line of discontinuity, of juxtaposing tectonic plates where there had previously been solid, unbroken ground (Baxter Magolda and King 2004; Parks 2011; Pizzolato 2005).

A student's state of readiness or openness to change sets the stage for his or her response to and growth from disorientation, the focus of this chapter. Within that context, the student is exposed to new and possibly disturbing realities or viewpoints and encouraged to engage in them intellectually and emotionally. This involvement must be strong enough and long enough to carry the student into the next phase of transformation, the arduous process of reflecting analytically on underlying values and beliefs.

Ready or Not . . .

New college students often thrill at, and worry about, the variety of courses available, the chance to make new friends, and the opportunity to live independently. They know they will experience some changes during the next four years. Michael Bumbry, like many of his peers, described this feeling of being on the cusp of something new when he went to college: "I think it's probably cheesy or cliché, but I hope that everyone anticipates changing in some way. What that is exactly, I don't think anyone can predict. I anticipated changing. What that meant for me, I had no clue."

While many students expect to *encounter* "different," they don't expect to *become* different. Students expect to try some fun new things and be exposed to new ideas and environments, but they often do not anticipate that these experiences will change them in any fundamental—or even uncomfortable—way. These changes are expected merely to add an interesting new dimension or layer to their existing sense of who they are.

Recognizing these common undergraduate attitudes, college faculty and staff can take steps to help students become more open and ready for change, ready even for transformation. Knowing the types of students your college tends to enroll can help you anticipate and plan for their readiness levels. Do new students typically lean toward challenge, or do they shy away? Do students seem to become more, or less, open to challenge and change in their time at your college? While student attitudes and behaviors are shaped by what they bring to college, their readiness for transformation can also be encouraged or discouraged by an institution's culture, programs, and people.

Take Michael Bumbry, for example, who, from the day he enrolled at Elon, jumped at the opportunity to get involved in new and demanding activities. Before he even arrived on campus, he picked a first-year housing option that would challenge him—a living-learning community focused on service learning. During his first week on campus, he ran for and was elected vice president of his class. The second week, he auditioned for an Elon television show called *Straight Talk*. From the start, he was ready to stretch himself and welcomed many overlapping challenges.

Students like Michael can be easy to spot. Working with students preparing for study abroad courses, Richard McBride, Elon's chaplain emeritus, says, "The ones that I predict are going to be engaged are the ones who are asking lots of questions about the new culture we are entering. They're inquisitive about the culture and the social norms of the new place, how to honor them and respect them, and not violate them." But, cautions McBride, "I have been wrong; I don't always read it right. Faculty and staff are often surprised by which students end up being deeply changed by their college experiences."

Whether we can spot them easily or not, some students need more priming for change than others. To help all students, but particularly those who are more hesitant or disengaged, there is value in making the educational process transparent (Winkelmes 2013). Setting an overt expectation of change, of some upheaval, and of discomfort promotes an awareness of what is involved in the transformative process and prompts a better appreciation for its outcome.

As Deborah Long tells her students, "If you are the same person at the end of this semester that you are right now, then neither one of us has done our job." Michael Bumbry agrees. "I think it's certainly appropriate even to tell our campus tour groups when they come through Admissions, 'Expect to be enriched, expect to be challenged, expect to think about things that perhaps you never considered.'" These sentiments echo what Ken Bain (2004) reports in his research on "the best" college teachers: "the key to understanding the best teaching can be found not in particular practices or rules but in the *attitudes* of the teachers, in their *faith* in their students' abilities, in their *willingness* to take their students seriously and to let them assume control of their own education" (78, emphasis in original). These excellent teachers, Bain concludes, offer students both a commitment to high standards and an explicit confidence in each student's capacity to learn and grow.

Setting those expectations can be tricky, though. While students know they will learn a lot of disciplinary content in college, they don't necessarily think they need or want to transform as individuals. In fact, students spend the whole admissions process telling us just how great they are as-is. Implying or stating that all students will, even must, change can be perceived as something of an affront, as if we were implying that there is something inherently wrong with them as individuals when they come to us. Sometimes, Richard McBride reminds us, a student comes along and says, "I'm very happy with who I am; I don't want to change. Why would I? I am perfectly comfortable and things are good. Life is good; I just want to get a degree." But even these students may find themselves engaged in deeper questions somewhere along the way when they are immersed in an environment that is rich with stimulation and are surrounded by peers who are embracing the journey.

Setting expectations begins with a university's marketing and admissions staff. Hearing stories from those who have emerged on the other side of transformation, building anticipation, can help open students to the opportunities that await them. An institution can also select for those students who seem poised for significant growth, though it is equally valuable to invite into the community those who have yet to reach that place and to help ready them for important change. Either way, it is important for colleges to know how best to work with both kinds of students.

On the one hand, students who are primed for change, in college or before they even come to us, are likely to respond to deeper, more intense challenges. On the other hand, some students might find such experiences more traumatic than transformative. They may become more open only after they successfully encounter the initial mild disorientations of college. As Michael Paige, a scholar of intercultural competence, has said, "Some students really do need to feel comfortable at 'taco night' in the dining hall before they can begin to contemplate studying abroad" (personal correspondence, August 2013). That's why it's important to offer a variety of experiences over the undergraduate years. For instance, some leap into Elon's Gap Semester program that immerses a cohort of first-year students in a semester's worth of intellectual, cultural, and physical challenges—from a three-week wilderness excursion in the Rocky Mountains to a six-week home-stay with a family in Costa Rica. Other students, however, cannot imagine diving that deeply that fast; instead, they seek a homey spot in a dorm with peers who seem to be like them, only cautiously stepping out into experiences on campus that might force them to stretch and grow. Yet, after four years, students who take either of those paths, and many in between, can find themselves profoundly changed. There's no single recipe for transformation.

Keeping the expectation of transformation in front of faculty and staff can also help build a culture that reinforces it across an institution. This culture can inspire and embolden each of us to design spaces and activities appropriately, giving us the courage to hold steadfast through students' unsettled times or to support the struggle in the face of a pained student or an angry parent. It can keep our focus on the long-term benefit of transformation rather than on the short-term feel-good of easy comfort.

Designing Productively Disruptive Experiences

The college itself plays a critical role in purposefully disturbing the student's status quo, creating what may be a sometimes unexpected and even unwanted internal disorder. By designing intentional opportunities for productive disruptions, for students to encounter difference and to see the limits of their assumptions, we can facilitate the transformative experiences of our students.

Many things about college life can challenge a student. Perhaps he has to work harder to make the grades than he did in high school. Maybe her roommate is not the person she expected or wanted. Maybe the competition for a spot in the musical ensemble or the sports team is much fiercer than in the past. Maybe the laundry does not just do itself magically on the weekend.

Disorientation might start with seemingly small concerns, but transformation is about more dramatic shifts, challenges that break open previously unquestioned beliefs and call for them to be reconciled with new possibilities. The process begins when a person experiences some type of disorienting dilemma. The trigger for that disorientation can appear as a gradual unfolding or as an immediate crisis (Taylor 1998). A semester of struggle in a poetry course may slowly lead a student to question whether she can become a professional writer, or a friend's behavior at a late-night party might shock a student into asking, "Who are my friends, really— and who am I becoming?"

These challenges are essential to the transformative process, but for optimally positive outcomes, for the disruption to be *productive*, guidance and support are important. One of the tasks for college faculty and staff, therefore, is figuring out what is productive disorientation and what is overwhelming and destructive. Challenges that transform are ones that sharply but respectfully challenge students' values and assumptions about themselves and the world they live in. Dissonance at the level of belief or value is what changes and clarifies identity. Disruption that obliterates hope for new possibilities is not productive and should be, as much as possible, avoided. One of the fundamental tasks for colleges is to help students experience the appropriate amount of challenge at the appropriate time, staying within a student's zone of proximal development—stretching the student into discomfort without tearing him apart.

At the heart of this work, then, is the college's role in structuring and encouraging experiences that promote transformative learning. We cannot transform for students, nor can we create the perfect set of challenges guaranteed to produce transformation in every student. Students are diverse, making a paint-by-numbers approach to transformation impossible. Students also have choice and agency, granting them the capacity to act in ways that can be at once necessary for growth and potentially contrary to it. Because of its personal and open-ended nature, we cannot plan transformation. But we can plan *for* transformation by creating an environment that is conducive to it. We can:

- Go broad, creating opportunities across all aspects of college life and for all students;
- Go long, ensuring that opportunities continue to be threaded throughout the four years, not just as the student enters college or in a culminating experience; and
- Go deep, pushing past the surface and asking deeper, bigger questions and calling on students' best selves to handle honest, possibly tough, feedback that is respectfully delivered.

Going Broad to Engage All Students

At its most basic level, disorientation involves exposure to new and diverse things. It seems almost too obvious to say, but to get students to think differently, they must be exposed to differences—not only learning additional facts or honing certain skills but also colliding with different perspectives, different possible truths. An environment rich in diversity—a multiplicity of people, ideas, practices, and beliefs—increases the likelihood of both structured and informal opportunities to interrupt the familiar and the comfortable. These differences could come in the form of exposure to and discussion of new ideas; interactions with people of different races, ethnicities, genders, cultures, intelligences, political views, communication styles, values and goals, and so on; or taking on roles students have not previously seen themselves playing.

Eric Brown's disorientation began during his first week on campus, ironically during his orientation experience, one that aimed to make him feel comfortable at Elon but also left him unsettled in his new home: "I realized that I'm not as smart as I thought I was." In high school, Eric never questioned his ability to excel, but in college he found himself in contact with many talented and ambitious peers: "That made me think about how I had to change. I remember I just kept thinking, 'Dude, you're not as smart as you think you are. You need something else.'" His exposure to a broader variety of students pushed Eric to reach further, reenvisioning what he was capable of and recognizing the seriousness of the task before him; he was no longer back in his comfortable high school, and he needed to change to succeed in this new environment.

At Elon, as at every college, faculty design courses to incorporate new knowledge and different ways of looking at a topic and at the world. In particular, the core curriculum is intentionally designed to expose all students to new perspectives. As part of that core, all students are required to take "The Global Experience," a first-year seminar that examines individual responsibility from multiple perspectives. "Global," as students call it, explores implications created by cultural and natural diversity and the possibilities for human communication and cooperation within and across this diversity. Global also emphasizes student and faculty creativity through active and collaborative learning (Morris and Swing 2005).

Ben Smith is typical of many students when he recalled his experience of Global: "I think it was one of the first things that really made me recognize how big the world was and how much was going on in the world that I wasn't even aware of." Professor Jim Brown has taught the course for years, and he concurs: "It moves them in directions they haven't thought about before. The dissonance for them is that they realize the world isn't the way they thought it was; they are suddenly seeing things that they had no idea about, things that affect millions of people that they had no idea about. But in the exit interviews, students say that Global leaves one of the longest-lasting impressions of any course."

While Global may have a similar approach to other excellent first-year seminars at many colleges, "Reacting to the Past" creates an entirely different classroom dynamic. The historian Mark Carnes and his colleagues at Barnard College created *Reacting,* an immersive role-playing pedagogy designed for use in first-year seminars. In each *Reacting* "game," students spend weeks enacting the trial of Anne Hutchinson in colonial Massachusetts Bay or debating the correct application of Confucian tenets to a succession crisis in the Ming Dynasty. The philosophical ideas, the competition, and the group work at the heart of *Reacting* often spark intense student engagement. Carnes reports that after teaching his first *Reacting* game, he distributed Barnard's standard course evaluation form:

> One question left them flummoxed: "What could be done to encourage discussion?" "What does this mean?" one student scribbled on the form. "Students *are* the class." "The problem wasn't to get us to speak,

it was to get us to shut up," another wrote. "We didn't need encouragement," added another. "Tranquilizers would have been more in order."
(Carnes 2005, 10)

By pushing students into what Carnes calls "distant worlds" and giving
them a stake (including a portion of their course grade) in the outcome of
the game, *Reacting* plunges students into both historical and classroom
experiences that can be productively disorienting (Carnes 2011).

Academic experiences beyond the classroom also are an essential means
to "go broad" by prompting all students to experience disruption. At Elon,
for instance, all undergraduates must fulfill the Experiential Learning Requirement (ELR) by completing at least two of the following mentored experiences: leadership, study abroad, undergraduate research, service learning, and internships. By putting students into new, and often unfamiliar,
roles and contexts, each of these has the potential to be disruptive. Some
students encounter challenges on campus in a science lab while doing undergraduate research; others face it when immersed in a previously unknown
community while doing service or when required to make a leadership
decision that will spark controversy among their peers. Doing her communications internship in London, for instance, amplified the experience
for Olivia Hubert-Allen: "I think being in a different culture just sort of
helped throw me even more out of my loop. I think if I had been in an
American city, I wouldn't have been as disconnected socially from my
friends and family. I could have just called them on the phone whenever I
needed them."

Not all students encounter such challenges in their ELRs, but the university has built structures into the curriculum and the co-curriculum to
ensure each student experiences what George Kuh (2008) calls "high-impact
practices." Kuh explains that these educational activities are "unusually effective" at prompting student learning and growth for six reasons:

1. They require students to devote significant time and effort to
   educationally purposeful tasks.
2. They put students in circumstances that prompt substantive
   interactions with faculty and peers over an extended period of time.
3. They increase the likelihood that students will encounter diversity
   through contact with people who are different from themselves.

4. Students receive frequent feedback on their learning and performance.
5. Students have the opportunity to try out their learning in different contexts, often both on and off campus.
6. Students are encouraged to connect distinct academic and personal experiences to make meaning. (Kuh 2008, 14–17)

These high-impact characteristics are helpful guideposts for efforts to reach all students with productively disruptive experiences in college.

Going Long to Engage Students throughout College

To be most effective and to increase the likelihood that college will meet the transformative needs of its students, these eye-opening opportunities— opportunities to juxtapose the new against the old, the strange and unaccustomed to the safe and familiar—must be threaded throughout the four-year college experience. Colleges often focus on initial experiences for first-year students and culminating experiences for seniors, but in the sophomore and junior years the opportunities can be more haphazard, left to chance or to the student's initiative. McBride explains the implications of neglecting these students: "I think we need a continual awakening. I don't think we stay awake. I think we come back to our comfort zone, whatever it was, and we need repeated exposures or repeated awakenings until we get into that new habit."

The middle years of an undergraduate education are full of opportunities for challenge and growth. This is when many students commit to a major, cement friendships, make choices about experiences like study abroad, and begin to think concretely about life after college. At the same time, these students often have neither access to the programs offered to first years nor the comfort of a familiar declared major. And, frequently, students do not have the guidance and support from their families that they experience as they transition in and out of college. Sophomores commonly report feeling "invisible" or "lost," and only recently have scholars and practitioners begun to systematically study and support this "too often neglected population" of students (Hunter, Tobolowsky, and Gardner 2009, 2).

An increasing number of institutions are working to simultaneously support and challenge students during these decisive middle years of college. Elon, for instance, has created a series of "Transition Strategies" noncredit courses intended to help students navigate the many choices they face. Some of these courses focus on career opportunities for particular majors and the application process for national fellowships, but many of these seminars have a broader scope. "Living the Dream: Preparing to Go Global after Graduation," for example, is designed to support and inspire students who would like to live and work abroad after college. Faculty and staff who teach these courses often note how nervous many of their students are at the start of the term, since enrolling typically feels like a step out of the now-comfortable world of college and into the future. To emphasize the importance of that step, students register for these "Transition Strategies" seminars in the same way and at the same time that they sign up for academic courses.

Pitzer College in California takes a different, and perhaps more comprehensive, approach with its Sophomore Year Symposium. Beginning with a daylong conference open to all sophomores, this program extends through the year to encourage sophomores to engage with each other, with upper-class mentors, and with faculty and staff. Students are encouraged to think broadly about decisions they will face during the year and beyond. Monthly "Celebrating Sophomores" programs are held through the year to support students in exploring topics ranging from internships and study abroad to career planning.

Duke University's Sophomore Year Experience (SYE) aims to both empower and challenge students, emphasizing that during this year students "begin to take on added responsibilities and make decisions that will affect the rest of their lives" (Duke University Student Affairs, n.d.). More than programs at either Elon or Pitzer, Duke's program integrates academic and career-oriented elements with efforts to support student wellness. Duke also formally involves the Sophomore Class Council in the planning and implementation of SYE, underscoring the importance of students taking additional responsibility for their own learning and development as they progress through college.

The goal of each of these programs is to help students manage and integrate their learning from the many disruptions they encounter across their four years of college. Since we cannot know when a student will encounter the kind of dissonance that can spark transformation, we need to be—and we need to prepare them to be—open to struggle and change in the many transitions they will face throughout their undergraduate years.

Going Deep to Engage Meaning and Purpose

Students we interviewed who experienced deep changes faced a dissonance that went beyond simply involvement in a new experience. Mere exposure is not sufficient to ensure transformation. In fact, often the immediate response when encountering a new and uncomfortable way of looking at things is to pull away from it and resettle in one's previous view.

Instead, to be transformed, a student must move from exposure to engagement in the disorientation process. Faculty and staff can nudge students to move deeper. We can do that in many ways: talking patiently with students who are feeling disoriented, posing difficult follow-up questions when they seem too comfortable in a perspective, presenting an ill-structured problem that has no clear or easy answer, allowing students to make mistakes they can learn from, challenging them to perform to higher standards or in new roles, and providing candid feedback.

Pam Kiser, a long-time faculty advocate for and practitioner of service learning at Elon, notes:

> My experience in experiential learning is that experience itself can teach exactly the wrong thing . . . I remember a student who wrote in a paper, "I observed Criminal Court in Alamance County, and I learned that the crimes in Alamance County are pretty much committed by Blacks because everyone who came before the judge was Black." You read something like that and you think, "Hmmm, a little information deficit here. Let's talk some about how the legal process works, all the different screens the person goes through before they actually get to court, how people get diverted away who have resources, what their other paths are." . . . I have definitely seen problems when people assume that students—or any of us—are going to go out and learn purely from experience, without the benefit of some intentionally directed knowledge that sheds light on that experience.

Questions that go beyond the surface of an experience call students to invest more heavily in the transformative process. Being pushed to analyze experiences, respond to feedback, and ask themselves questions that lie at the heart of complex issues help students to go deeper into discomfort and disorientation. But it is sometimes not easy to get students to probe so deeply into what they think and feel about an issue; not surprisingly, students often shy away from difficult or confusing situations, no matter how much we would like them to lean into them. Students bring to college habits of schooling that may rely on skillfully receiving information and returning it to the instructor in the expected way. (Indeed, college admissions processes, and perhaps some of our own courses, may reward just such behavior.) Asking hard questions and being willing to struggle with not knowing may be fundamentally new experiences for some students, even (or perhaps especially) for our most academically accomplished ones. Faculty and staff should gently but persistently invite students into such a liminal space, at the same time remembering how awkward we all can feel when we are destabilized.

To do just that, English professor Jean Schwind likes to pose questions that even she does not have the answers to:

> One of my goals in a class is for me to leave the class knowing something or thinking something that I didn't know or think when I went in. When I hear something from students that strikes me as odd or unusual or that I haven't considered before, I will say so. I'll ask them to elaborate, and I'll tell them why I haven't thought about that. I will send them an e-mail afterward: "I wish you would think more about this for Thursday's class because it's really percolating in my brain." I want to let them know when they've gotten my mental gears going.

Giving students increasing responsibility is another means of deepening disorientation in a way that shifts a student's self-perceptions. "Elon Experiences" are replete with opportunities for students to take on responsibility and leadership roles inside the classroom and out. Working one-on-one with faculty members on research projects, doing internships, and service learning efforts (connecting classroom learning with societal issues while working in the community) are just some of the contexts in which students can design and carry out projects for which they bear the chief responsibility.

Hendrix College in Arkansas does just that by framing its experiential learning requirement as the Odyssey Program. Hendrix faculty defined six categories of engaged learning: "artistic, global, professional and leadership internships, service, undergraduate research, and special projects that don't fit in the other categories" (Reed 2013, 33). Students must earn credits in at least three of those categories to graduate. The Odyssey Program complements this curricular requirement by supporting efforts by faculty and staff to develop integrative experiences and to help students chart their own courses through these experiences. One Hendrix student with a passion for working with homeless people, for example, linked service and internship opportunities with academic study of intentional communities to create an interdisciplinary major for herself in urban studies and justice (Reed 2013, 34). By using the metaphor of an odyssey, this program emphasizes the centrality of students in constructing their own paths through the rich and challenging environment of college.

Another way of drawing students deeper into this reordering phase of transformative learning is by providing feedback on more than simply the final product. Although it may sometimes be uncomfortable, students benefit tremendously from well-timed critical feedback. What they most often want from their mentors and teachers is respect, support, and challenge. Affirmation feels good, but to learn and develop they need to be prompted to focus not only on their successes but also on their struggles. Unfortunately, in many instances faculty give students limited or detail-oriented feedback, either too busy or too cautious to really engage with student work. Students notice this. Jill Medhus, for instance, says she wishes there were more direct feedback from professors. "I don't think that writing comments on a paper is enough. I think we really need to hear it from the professor's mouth. If professors and students both would make an effort to make appointments, and if the professor would say, 'It's all right that you didn't do this thing well, but here is how I would like you to correct it so you can progress in the future,' I think that it would be a growth opportunity for professors as well as students. That's what we are here for at Elon, to grow."

We asked Jill if she had experienced people demanding more of her than she was comfortable with. "Definitely. That's necessary. But mostly I think I have the opposite problem where people won't tell me that I am not doing enough until it is too late. That just hurts because I would have been able to transform into a better person or at least be better at what I intended to do, been more aware of myself, if they had given me that feedback. I think there have been more situations where I haven't gotten enough feedback on something negative, maybe because people are afraid to give negative feedback."

Olivia Hubert-Allen gives an example of feedback that was difficult but ended up making a difference for her.

> I had a writing professor in the School of Communications in an intro media writing course, and we had to cover a meeting to write a story. She had this really strict policy about, "You can't have excuses, blah blah blah," But I had written for the local *Times News* and had covered a couple of meeting stories already, and I already had some clips. So I sort of had this idea, "Maybe I can get out of it." I had a conflict on the night I was supposed to go, something I thought was more important. I wrote her and said, "I've already written this story a couple of times. Can I just show you those?" She wrote me back this really mean e-mail that was, like, "No. You are not getting out of this assignment. I can't even believe you asked." I actually cried. I was, like, "Oh no, did I offend her? I just wanted to see if I could get out of this." I went to the town meeting and covered the story, and I ended up doing great on the assignment. I submitted it to the *Times News,* and they published it. It was a good experience for me. It taught me that I couldn't mess around with her. It also taught me to make time for things. I ended up being able to do both things I had that night. I had to write quickly to make the story work, and I was on a tight deadline. It was a little tough love.

The Challenge of Failure

Both Jill and Olivia's stories underscore the importance of risk and even failure in the disorientation process. Students like Jill and Olivia typically come to college quite practiced at minimizing or hiding failure. Occasions on which they experience failure of some magnitude can be unnerving and can call their very identities into question. One student at Elon who started with the goal of medical school confronted this issue in his first semester biology course: "The first test was really bad. I studied a lot for it. It wasn't multiple choice or anything, and it was really hard because it was a lot of material to cover in such a short amount of time. I studied even more for the second test and I really thought I did better, but I actually did worse. That's when I knew that it wasn't going to work out in the end." He eventually graduated as a successful theater student, and upon reflection he credited that biology course with helping him better understand who he wanted to be—rather than who he felt he was expected to be.

While faculty and staff might reasonably hesitate to expose too many students to full-on failures such as this student describes, opportunities exist for micro-failures, experiences in which smaller efforts do not pan out but which, if recovery is made, do not jeopardize the overall goal. The goal here is not failure, per se, but approximated failure, what knowledge management expert Dave Snowden (2012) calls "safe-to-fail" experiences. Biology professor Linda Niedziela offers a simple example from her lab, telling of her own struggles, and even failures, to create a safer space for students to take risks. "I'll tell them, 'Okay, you've never done this and I have; you've never set a hood on fire and I have.' That's saying the professor is not infallible. We're all are taking our foundation of knowledge and we're building on it; no one is perfect and no one knows everything." Niedziela also intentionally encourages students to become increasingly independent in her lab. When one advanced undergraduate struggled with his thesis research, she provided lots of support in the lab at first but then gradually found ways to step away in order to make him take more responsibility: "He often said, 'Dr. N what should I do now?' I've told him, 'This is great, you trust me a whole lot, but we want this to be a partnership here.' He's having real difficulty with that. But just this morning, it was a bad day in the lab, nothing was working right. He needed me immediately and wasn't sure I'd be in, so he had to make a decision. He later walked into my office and said, 'Dr. N, I made an executive decision.' And then he explained what he had done. I laughed and said, 'That is exactly what I want you to do. It really is!'"

Niedziela sees the willingness to take intellectual and personal risks as a central challenge for disorientation:

In general most students struggle with that. It is really hard for them to have to think it through enough, because they don't trust themselves. What I have found with a lot of Elon students is that they are really great students, they are really smart. And they hate failure. They hate the idea of looking silly or foolish or not doing it right. So this idea that they could actually make a mistake, especially with something they've put their heart and soul into like a research project or a final class project, is really tough for them. But when you turn it on them, "Well, you're the one who should know, not me," is when you start seeing them be willing to struggle and really learn. That's when they really start understanding the education process, I think.

Failure alone, of course, is not inherently transformative; it must be processed to yield its benefits. Faculty and staff must walk a fine line between helping students redeem their experiences by learning from them and rescuing them from the consequences of their choices. A key component of this art of contextualizing failure is redefining success as a measure of internal growth rather than as simply external awards and achievements. As educators we recognize a kind of failure that goes far beyond an F on a transcript— such as when a student emerges from four years of college without engaging in significant struggle and growth. This kind of missed opportunity is not just unfortunate for the student; it also represents a form of failure for her college. If our mission is to transform students, then we should hold ourselves accountable when we fall short of our aspirations just as we proudly trumpet our success stories.

Balancing Challenge and Support

Given that the disorientation phase of transformative learning is both necessary and disconcerting, those of us in higher education need to think carefully about how to help students face these challenges with support, in particular the type of support that promotes transformation. As much as possible, the nature of the disruptive encounter must be intentionally constructed. Social hazing or incoherent teaching, for example, are disruptive forces that are not likely to yield positive results. In and out of the classroom, challenges should be designed and tailored to move each student forward in the transformative process.

This requires more than light, friendly challenges. We must guide students toward deeper levels of disorientation that are often accompanied by upheaval, frustration, and even distress. Students rarely expect this level of turmoil. Amy, like many of her peers, was eager for college. She recalls, "I knew it was going to be unlike anything I had experienced before. . . . Many times in high school, I didn't feel that challenged, so I was super eager to get to college and be surrounded by people who also wanted to learn, particularly with Honors, because I knew I would be around people who were really enthusiastic about learning and just experiencing things and taking it all in." What she did not expect was the painful shifts to her previous way of looking at the world that she experienced in some of her classes—the pain that brought about the tearful conversation that opened this chapter—which she now recognizes as a necessary and valuable part of her growth and maturation.

In her interview, Bre Detwiler was asked a version of the question that many skeptics pose when appraising the transformative potential of the four-year college experience: "Would you have changed just as much if, instead of attending Elon, you had spent the same four years living on your own in the woods?" Not surprisingly, she said no. Her reason for the "no," however, is revealing. "I think some of my transformation has come from challenges to what I believe in. If I were just in the woods, I would be talking to myself and just reaffirming that I was right. Maybe I would feel closer to the earth or something," she laughed, "but I think opposition is really key for my transformation and the opening of my eyes, or hearing something I really didn't like and didn't want to think about. . . . In the woods, I would probably just keep thinking what I already thought. That was part of why I didn't see a lot of transformation in high school, which I think are also potentially transformative years. I wasn't being challenged. Everybody told me, 'Yeah, you're right.' I was, like, 'Yeah, I *am* right!' instead of, 'You are completely wrong; you don't know what you are talking about. Go figure it out.'"

Maggie Spingler's comment echoes Bre's experience, emphasizing the feelings that accompany this challenge. "You realize that you can't defend what you used to think was true. It's a little bit frustrating, I guess—frustrating and confusing because you're not really sure where to go from there. Everything is up in the air. You don't know what to believe and what to think. It's kind of a weird place to get stuck in until you start to look at it and start forming new opinions."

Creating this kind of dissonance carries an inherent tension, of course. Transformation requires disruption and destabilization, but there's a balance to be struck. Too little challenge, and nothing ever changes. Too much challenge, and the person is overwhelmed and retreats back into the familiar, perhaps more determined than ever to stay there. The support that allows students to sustain the challenge is founded in respect. It's not about fixing or removing the source of the frustration or distress. It's not about making it easier. It's about expressing respect for the depth and seriousness of what the student is experiencing. And about validating it—letting them know it's supposed to be this way. It's "right" even though it feels "wrong." It's not protection from but rather support through.

Maggie chose to come to Elon because it "felt comfortable." Larissa Ferretti expresses a similar sentiment: "I think when you're looking to where you are going to college—for me, I was looking where I was going to be most comfortable. I wasn't looking for, 'Where am I going to change and be uncomfortable?' No. When I'm going twelve hours from home, I want to feel comfortable and have people that are nice and have nice facilities and all that stuff. That was what I was looking for, so I found that in Elon. When you get here, that's when you really realize what is happening." Yet after she arrived on campus, she began to stretch. "It's scary. Anytime that I have felt that—you feel a little feeling in your stomach. You're really uneasy, and you're not really sure that's what you want to do. That's what I felt when I was coming to Elon, moving really far away. That is what I felt when I started doing research with my psychology professor, Maureen Vandermaas-Peeler. You feel a little scared."

Olivia Hubert-Allen did not step into disorientation eagerly. "I think that for me personally I had to be pushed out of my comfort zone. I had a couple of professors who asked me to do things that I was kind of, like, 'Oh, God, there is no way!' I hated them at the time, but I knew from high school and past teachers I have had that what they were doing was good and it was for a reason. I think for me personally . . . I don't think you can be babied through the transformation process. I kind of needed tough love and I got that in a couple of places."

Sometimes students are not the ones who are most resistant to change; sometimes it's the parents. Professor Pam Kiser recounted the story of being in a session with the parents of incoming first-year students. A father raised his hand and said, "I want you to address my concern that I don't want my daughter's religion—I don't want people messing with that. I want to be reassured that no one will challenge my daughter on her beliefs or values." Kiser told us "My thought was to say, 'That's what you're paying us for.' But I think a better, a more thoughtful response would have been, 'I want to assure you that your daughter's beliefs and values will be respected. In any classroom, I hope and believe she will find an environment most of the time that really seeks diversity of points of view. We are not in the business of taking beliefs and values from anybody, but we are in the business of exploring all of that. She will probably encounter views very different from her own, but, no, we won't try to take those away from her.' As a parent myself, I would feel if my child went through four years of college and I did not see anything at the end of those four years but the same person with a diploma in her hand, I would be wanting a refund."

As Kiser's story suggests, faculty and staff also can be uncomfortable and stressed when their students are struggling with disorientation. We need to learn to be okay with our students—and even their parents— being deeply disoriented, scared, frustrated, and yes, unhappy. Contemporary American culture certainly equates support with unconditional affirmation. As news anchor Brian Williams joked at Elon's 2013 graduation, "I sometimes expect to hear a parent say: "Great job breathing today, son, here's a trophy." While we may laugh at some of the excess, we perhaps should not laugh too loudly on campuses replete with high grades and innumerable award ceremonies. Indeed, there is a certain allure to all of this praise of students. Not only do students feel good when they get this affirmation, but so do we. We think, "I must be a good teacher (or resident advisor, or parent, or . . .) if my students are so great."

However, our interview data confirm what researchers have found: Students need most to know that we believe they can do difficult things, and that we respect, care for, and value them even as they struggle (Cole 2008). When asked what it is about being valued that contributes to transformation,

Michael Bumbry responded, "I would say it means that someone cares . . . when you feel appreciated or recognized, not necessarily in a big public 'Let's clap for Michael Bumbry way,' but a sort of, 'We see what you are doing. This is great. Keep up the good work,' . . . that gives you the motivation to do good things."

With that authentic validation, students feel more capable of reaching and achieving, which is the foundation of self-esteem. Becky Olive-Taylor, Elon's associate dean of Academic Support, sees this in her work each day. The nature of her role at Elon has given her a view of students in crisis, perhaps more than most people get. "I think that when you support someone, you basically have that tough conversation to explain what, from your perspective, you see is happening here. You confront an individual with the behaviors that are keeping them mired in one place; you have that tough conversation, whereas when you enable someone, you never really have that tough conversation. You figure out how to address the crisis and move on to the next thing." She continues, "I suppose in an ideal world, we would all have such perfect radar that we could tell when students needed us to prod and when they needed us to back off, but we don't live in an ideal world." Yet choosing never to have those conversations is, in Dean Olive-Taylor's mind, "a cover for 'I don't have to examine whether what I'm doing is supporting transformational learning.'" We should put ourselves "somewhere in the middle, where it's clear what the opportunities are that are up to the student, and what the expectations are that are part of this community."

English professor Jean Schwind puts this most simply: "Students don't really need support unless you're challenging them. You don't need support to do the easy stuff; you can do that on your own." "Part of support for me," she explains, "is just letting the students know that they are interesting people and they are worth thinking about and responding to. Then they will think about what they're thinking themselves." When we validate students' experiences of discomfort and frustration, we help them frame their experience, making them aware of the transformative process itself. We help them step back from the immediacy of the emotions and see the larger picture, recognize the feelings as an inherent part of a desirable growth process. As we do this, we not only help them move forward with their current situation but help them transfer this awareness to future growth.

Incidents beyond Our Control

No matter how carefully we design our academic programs and attend to the dynamics of the living environment, unintended disruptive events can and will occur. A student can get stranded in an airport for days while studying abroad, get robbed while away on an internship, or have a family member die suddenly. Our ability to support students through times like this helps them emerge from the experience relatively unscathed and better equips them to learn from and deal with similar unexpected life events in their future.

Sometimes there are other kinds of calamities that go far beyond these kinds of ordeals, shaking all of us to the core. When we asked Jill, a senior, to tell us what had led to the new sense of herself that she developed during her time in college, she spoke glowingly about her experiences in the Leadership Program and about her time as a member of a national student residence hall organization (RSA). "It was just amazing for me. I went to a conference last summer with RSA. I presented a program at the national conference, and I filled the room. It won a Top 40 Program award. . . . I've really seen a lot of growth in myself in that organization. I started out as a committee member, went into the PR position my sophomore year, was campus relations director this past year, and now I am going to be president this coming year."

"It sounds like this transformation has been pleasant and enjoyable," we remarked. Her answer to that simple remark changed the nature of our interview. "For some things, yes, for others, no," she replied, suddenly quieter. "I'm going to go into something that is really uncomfortable for me, but it has come to be a lot of who I am at Elon." She then told us that, even before she attended her first class on campus, a fellow student raped her during first-year orientation. "I didn't think I would ever get over that," she said. The orientation program included information about sexual violence, but in her new and vulnerable social situation, Jill did not initially tell anyone on campus about the assault. "I told some friends from back home. I told my mom so that she could get me an appointment to have testing. I didn't want to tell anyone at Elon because I thought they would see me differently, especially because he and I had a lot of mutual friends. And that would be weird."

As she struggled to cope with this assault during her first year, Jill's grades suffered and she was dismissed from the Honors program. Eventually, however, Jill took an English class in which she was asked to write a reflection on, "What has changed you the most at Elon?" She knew immediately: "That was it," she said. "There's nothing that compares to that; it has tainted every experience I've had so far." Jill's English professor, Jean Schwind, had taught her "Global" course during Jill's first year. "I knew that she was an advocate for equal rights, women, all of that stuff," said Jill. "I didn't think that she would be somebody who would shun me. I really felt that she was somebody I could trust." After Jill submitted her paper, Professor Schwind emailed almost immediately. "She said, 'There are resources here. Nobody else has to know about it.' She did an amazing job. She directed me to the right people on campus and set me up with a local agency. Now I've become an advocate for sexual assault awareness. . . . I'm doing my final Common Good Project in the Leadership Program based on that experience. It is really amazing because most people after that happens either drop out or transfer. That didn't happen to me, and it's because of the support of the community that I had here."

The reality of college life—of life anywhere—is that tragedies occur. Students sometimes experience violent assaults, traumatic accidents, and the death of friends. Faculty and staff who shared the experience of September 11 with students on a college campus or who were there to counsel students after campus violence or during a natural disaster know the unspeakable distress and suffering that students—and all of us—can face (Huston and DiPietro 2007). As much as we want to avoid these experiences, they are a reality for our students and we must be prepared to deal with them. We may not be in control, but we still must guide our students through the pain and confusion.

A common theme from these diverse experiences is the importance of cultivating community. Social expressions of grief can be a way of coping with grief, and "recovery requires a sense of social community in which people feel supported in looking back and forward" (Eyre 2006, 454, quoted in Wesener, Peska, and Trevino 2010, 116). Candlelight vigils and other opportunities for silent yet communal reflection have become a familiar ritual. After the mass shooting at Virginia Tech, the university created an online public journal that invited community members to write condolences and reflections, yielding some 36,000 entries. No matter the particular format, effective responses to crisis "balance respect for the victims, honor the resilience of the survivors, and recognize the hope" for a better tomorrow (Wesener et al. 2010, 118).

When something horrible happens, how can we take the wisdom we have learned from other circumstances, other difficulties, so that the students can use this disruption, however terrible, to move forward? We believe that the skills—both theirs and ours—learned through planned challenges and intentional disorientation can help us respond in the most healing and effective way. The more adept college faculty and staff become at helping students work through the intentional transformative learning process, the better they will be able to help them respond to such hardships. As Jill remarked, "You never know what's going to happen and that's part of it, it really is. The good things and the bad things, you never know. The assault is obviously a bad thing, but it has become a good thing because I've given back a lot."

In meeting, processing, and surmounting disorienting challenges, students' views of themselves begin to change; they see themselves as increasingly able to deal with what life brings, to be resilient. That is the ultimate preparation for life. Our hope is that the graduates of our institutions will respond to unexpected and sometimes tragic events in ways that will eventually make themselves stronger, more confident, and better able to contribute to the good of the world. This, then, is the job of the college: to design and engage students in experiences that expose them to new and different ways of looking at the world and that challenge tightly held values, assumptions, and beliefs, and guide them through with transformative intention.

We cannot be satisfied that just some of our students are transformed on our campuses each year. There is more work to be done. We need to learn more about the process so we can expand this experience to more of our students. We should talk with and perhaps even study these students to see how they managed their disorientation and why they successfully crossed a threshold into a new place; at the same time, we should try to understand why many other students did not make similar transitions. Although transformation cannot be scripted, it need not be a random or hit-or-miss proposition. Well-designed experiences can facilitate openness—can stimulate curiosity, impart courage, make students more willing to stretch. We can be intentional about creating and valuing dissonance in higher education.

We need to better understand the dynamics between fomenting a sense of security and a willingness to take risks. As students repeatedly made clear in our interviews, having a sense of "home" gives them not only a safe haven to retreat to but also a place from which to step out into foreign territory and to explore new things. With this established "home," they can entertain disorientation. Stability affords them a measure of instability, an essential element in the transformative process.

CHAPTER THREE

Thinking It Through

"I would say just 'confusion.' It was a state of confusion," Stephanie Badavis recalls of her return to campus after a trip to Guatemala building a house with Habitat for Humanity. Stephanie, who had traveled frequently with her family growing up, did not expect the Habitat experience to be life changing. "I was excited about doing the Habitat house, but I think my expectations were really low compared with what I got out of it. I realized that this was absolutely different from anything I had ever seen."

The disorientation created by immersion in such a different culture, however, by itself was not enough to create lasting change in Stephanie's life. Transformation emerged as she continued to reflect on the experience afterward. "I couldn't stop talking about it for a month. And it was difficult because people didn't understand. I would describe to them what I saw and to them it was just another poor area and another city. To me it was something completely different."

Stephanie's intense need to talk out her experience illustrates a vital element of transformative learning—the pivotal role of critical reflection. Long ago, John Dewey (1997) noted that experience alone isn't educative; only when experience is paired with reflection is learning likely to occur and to last. It's no surprise that institutions of higher education seek to foster critical thinking and reflective practices in their students. We want to encourage our students not simply to think different thoughts but also to think those thoughts differently. The intention is not to eradicate particular conclusions, although this is sometimes a concern for both students and parents. Instead, the goal is learning and embracing the process of thinking carefully, analytically, and empathically, which may result in taking up new perspectives or recommitting to prior conclusions and beliefs.

With students engaging in daily classroom discussions and writing countless papers, reflection might seem so common in higher education that it barely merits discussion. However studies like Richard Arum and Josipa Roksa's *Academically Adrift* (2011) suggest that students are not learning as much, or as consistently, in college as we might want or assume. Recent research from the Wabash National Study demonstrates that "reflective learning was found to have a unique positive association with first-year growth in both critical-thinking skills and the need for cognition [e.g., inclination to inquiry and pursue life-long learning] . . . [and also] a significant positive link with four-year growth in critical thinking skills" (Pascarella and Blaich 2013).

Research also reveals that critical examination of the assumptions underlying our current ways of seeing and being in the world is at the core of the transformative process (Taylor 1998). In fact, in her examination of undergraduate students, Sabra Brock (2011) found reflection to be the most consistent predictor of self-reported transformative learning. As Paulo Freire (1970) asserted long ago, "An act of learning can be called transformative only if it involves a fundamental questioning and reordering of how one thinks or acts" (139). Sharan Merriam (2004) concurs: "Having an experience is not enough to effect a transformation. . . . What is valuable is not the experience itself but the intellectual growth that follows the process of reflecting on experience. Effective learning follows not from a positive experience but from effective reflection" (62).

Some students may be practiced at reflection when they arrive at college, although even the most skilled will benefit from continued guidance (King and Kitchener 1994). To other students, reflection may feel like a foreign process. It is certainly not intuitive for everyone, especially at this developmental stage, and students may not even recognize it as a valuable component of the learning process. The good news is that this fundamental skill can be learned. With instruction and encouragement, all students can develop their abilities to critically examine their underlying beliefs and assumptions when they find them challenged. Like any learned skill, however, critical reflection must be practiced. This chapter is about recognizing and fostering this process when it is happening and facilitating it when it is not.

The Nature of Critical Reflection

Critical reflection involves dismantling previously held thought and belief constructions, examining them from different perspectives, and then reconstructing them in a considered way. People typically are not aware of their assumptions until something disrupts the ordinary flow of things, making new or alternate vistas available to see. Until one notices an underlying belief as an assumption, it has no edges to define it, no contrasts to delineate it from what is normal and expected. Seeing a belief as *one* way of thinking prompts the realization that there must be *other* ways of thinking. Articulation then allows these new possibilities to be examined and, perhaps, brought together in a broader, more comprehensive view, a characteristic Jack Mezirow (1995) identifies as inclusivity. This integration process aids students in making meaning in ways that can persist, which is the very essence of transformative learning.

External Dialogue
Critical Reflection and Questioning

Critical reflection in the transformative process can be distinguished from mere reflection by its depth and its essential process of analysis and integration, of breaking apart and bringing together (Brookfield 2012). The nature of critical reflection is to go beyond the surface and to dig deep. The mode may look different in chemistry than in poetry or in a dorm room, but, regardless of the discipline or location, the process takes the student below the surface, excavating previously unrecognized assumptions. Although rational analysis has traditionally received the most attention in the literature, it is not the only means that can facilitate transformation. As Robert Boyd has noted, the transformative process also allows for intuitive reflection and the search for transcendent truth (Boyd 1991; Boyd and Myers 1988). John Dirkx (2003), too, calls for "soul work" in the reflective process. Regardless of whether reflection is understood and experienced as entirely rational or more capacious, dialogue is one of the most commonly documented and researched modes of reflection in transformative learning (Baumgartner 2002; Freire 1970; Mezirow 1991, 2000; Taylor

2007). Both internal and external dialogue play an essential role in the critical reflection process.

Although external dialogue can take diverse forms from conversation to writing, questioning is perhaps the most common approach for confronting existing ways of thinking. As modeled by many great teachers since Socrates, questioning is an elicitative, rather than an informing method of teaching. For the type of learning we want for our students, the most effective questioning is provocative, moving past the simple yes or no questions to how and why and so what (Brookfield and Preskill 2005). In our interviews, Professor Pam Kiser noted that students are used to being asked questions, but they are most accustomed to the ones for which there are correct answers, that is, answers they have previously been given in the *in*formative mode of teaching as opposed to the *trans*formative mode. In the transformative environment, students are asked questions that there are no easy answers to or that perhaps only they know the answers to, creating situations that encourage students to go beyond giving rote or superficial answers and helping them to dig deeper in their learning process.

Sharon Parks (2011) persuasively argues that faculty and staff in higher education often do not ask college students the right kinds of questions. Parks' research suggests that many students come to college intensely curious about meaning and identity. "Where can I be creative and thrive?" "Does my society have a place for me?" "Does my life have place and purpose?" "Where do I put my stake in the ground and invest my life?" (42, 222) The problem, according to Parks, is not that we ask too many lower-order, informative questions in our classes and cocurricular programs but rather that we rarely if ever prompt and guide our students to explore what she calls their big questions and worthy dreams. When we ignore or even get in the way of considering those essential questions, students can become frustrated and disengaged. By failing to deal with these fundamental questions, we are missing a powerful opportunity for our students to make positive, significant, and lasting changes in their lives and in society.

Parks (2011) illustrates the potential for critical reflection on big questions by profiling students in a "Designing Your Life" course offered in the School of Design at Stanford University. This limited enrollment seminar guides students through thorough questioning about their future. One student, for instance, wrote at the beginning of the term: "I'm chronically challenged by my tendency to 'go with the flow' of things. As much as I enjoying being laid back and accepting, I'd also like to learn how to play a more active role in thinking up and executing a plan or vision for myself. I'd like to challenge the flow" (221). By the end of the course, after a series of critical dialogues with peers and faculty, students may find themselves with a new orientation toward their life after college. As one student notes: "I'm thousands of miles from where I thought I would end up. . . . It [the course] helped me find a set of problems that I would like to tackle . . . and kind of [gave me] the courage not only to seek out what I want . . . but my ability to be okay with that" (221).

Students bring questions about the future and about vocation to their college experience in part because they do not know what to do with them on their own. They often do not know how to make sense of their aspirations and seek an environment that will help them get to the next place, to cross a threshold of meaning and purpose. Those of us in higher education are missing a profound opportunity, and not fulfilling the mission of our institutions, if we allow students to pass four years with us without probing essential questions.

Feedback

Feedback is another valuable form of external dialogue. On the simplest level, the professor's guiding comments and the resident advisor's thoughtful critique provide students with feedback that helps them test the validity of their ideas and actions. To make direct critical feedback more tangible and helpful, students need to feel that not only their questions and comments, but their very selves, are being heard and responded to (Cole 2008). When Larissa Ferretti was asked what in her college experience contributed to her transformative experience, she identified her relationship with a faculty mentor in undergraduate research and the feedback process in particular. "Dr. Vandermaas-Peeler and I have a really good relationship. She pushes me to think harder on things. When I had to do my thesis proposal, I wrote it all and I thought it was decent, and then she red-marked the whole thing. She's comfortable enough with me to push me to think beyond myself or beyond the subject matter. Not that I wasn't frustrated by that red-marking, but I know it's for a good cause."

The individual's recognition of the transformative learning process as an experience shared by others is an aspect Mezirow (1995) considered essential and that others including Lisa Baumgartner (2002) have since corroborated. The shared process of dialogue is a natural means of connecting with others to make meaning. The seeker is not alone but rather connects with and receives feedback from his community and, in fact, is often pushed or jarred by others who are also seeking answers. Professor Kiser remarks that in experiential learning classes, an environment in which students suddenly find themselves faced with a very different way of looking at the world, "the process needs to be thought and rethought and talked out with other people." There is considerable value, Kiser stresses, in sustained dialogue about difference, in striving to really hear one another. "It's about them telling their stories and figuring out where to go from there."

College faculty and staff can build the kinds of feedback that emerge from reflective dialogue into classwork, but, of course, students do not limit their selection of dialogue companions to the classroom. Remember Stephanie who wanted to talk to everybody about her experience with Habitat for Humanity in Guatemala? Student Rainey Bezila also recalled a number of people she engaged to process her changes—her mother, her roommate, and a mentor who directs the university's Center for Service Learning and Community Engagement. For 21-year-old Eric Brown, struggling with his experiences in a religious-based campus organization, some of his most effective dialogues took place over the phone with his twin brother, as each played devil's advocate for the other. The shared process allows the individual to step out of an immediate, personal awareness of dissonance and connect to a larger context from which to examine his or her feelings and assumptions. This expanded perspective facilitates the learner's ability to connect to a larger purpose or goal, a hallmark of the nature of change associated with transformation.

Internal Dialogue

Although the advantages of external dialogue in community are clear, internal dialogue, a kind of contemplative practice, can also be an effective path to transformation. Indeed, one of the purposes of college is to help students develop the capacity to reflect internally. Internal dialogue can be written or spoken, or simply imagined, with the self as the sole audience. In our interviews, students recounted their internal dialogues as occurring in personal journals, on long runs, and in quiet moments throughout the day. Research demonstrates that journaling, meditation, life narratives, and creative writing in a variety of disciplines are some of the modes of internal dialogue and critical reflection shown to be valuable in the transformative process (Carter 2002; Hunt 2013; King 2004).

Faculty and staff are finding a myriad of ways to integrate "contemplative pedagogies" into the undergraduate years. At Amherst College, for instance, physicist Arthur Zajonc and art historian Joel Upton team teach a course titled "Re-imagining the Human in a Technological Age." The course blends traditional academic study of Enlightenment, Romantic, and contemporary thinkers with extensive service alongside residents of a nearby Camphill community of adults with disabilities. Throughout the course, Zajonc and Upton introduce students to contemplative practices that ask "students to become conscious of the ways their habits of mind and the structure of their imagination shaped their experience in the world" (Palmer and Zajonc, 2010, 109). As the course concludes, after many students have become both increasingly skilled at contemplative practices and personally close to residents at Camphill, Zajonc and Upton prompt students to re-imagine what it means to be human. Many students reflect on how they understand themselves and their world in fundamentally different ways as a result of the course, asking "Why couldn't Amherst be more like Camphill?" (Palmer and Zajonc 2010, 112).

The Libby Residential Academic Program (LRAP) at the University of Colorado, Boulder, uses similar approaches toward a different goal. LRAP is a living-learning community for first- and second-year students in the arts. Both the program's interdisciplinary courses and its many co-curricular experiences are infused with contemplative practices. As Professor Deborah J. Haynes explains, "teaching students techniques of awareness, concentration, and means of disciplining their attention is absolutely essential in our era of fragmentation, ever-increasing speed, multitasking, and continuously interrupted attention" (Palmer and Zajonc 2010, 179).

By helping students cultivate skill in, and an orientation toward, inner dialogue, these programs and many others (e.g., Braskamp, Trautvetter, and Ward 2006) encourage students to be open to and capable of reflective learning. A psychotherapist friend used to refer to the "back pocket therapist" she hoped her clients would develop as they neared discharge status. It was a questioning habit that began as "What would my therapist say?" and evolved into "What do I say?" Similarly, once the inner dialoguing process is well practiced and students near graduation, we hope that they have developed a "back pocket mentor" who can accompany them throughout life.

Integration and Reconstruction

Identifying and connecting to a larger purpose or a sense of meaning is particularly important for the young adult, perhaps more so than for the adult learners with whom transformative learning was first investigated (Parks 2011). Deborah Long is professor of education and director of the Elon Academy, a college access and success program for academically promising high school students with strong financial need or no family history of higher education. She recalls the response of Christine Walton, an Elon undergraduate who worked with students in the Elon Academy, in her required reflection on the experience:

> She sent me, within a day, about a two-page-long reflection about how she had been transformed by her experience with the Elon Academy. It was powerful to read. The transformation was on so many different levels. On a very personal level she said that she had never been particularly interested in students who came from very challenging backgrounds; she just hadn't thought about it much. She said, "Now I want to devote my life to this because I realize I've had every opportunity and it's been easy for me. I realize how many people there are out there who don't have the same opportunities I have. I want to be part of making it possible for them to have what I've got."

This reflection process, though essential, is not guaranteed to happen among college students, even when they are exposed to new, diverse, and challenging experiences. Developmentally, we cannot count on students to be able to reflect analytically when they first arrive at college. Specificity is not a given either when students reflect on what they have done. "The trip was so great! I'll never be the same!" But then what? Students are capable of unpacking the suitcases they came home with, but they will need assistance unpacking their values and experiences as they learn to integrate their beliefs, actions, and identities.

One Elon student's complaints about her first-year history class illustrate the mind-set shared by some, perhaps many, of her peers: "I did not like my professor at all. He just had a different teaching style than I can handle. . . . It was not very much memorization. It was all in comprehending everything, taking it in, and knowing how to fit it into what is going on right now, comparing it to the past. It wasn't my thing." We can hope that, with repeated opportunities to do more critical thinking, such students will emerge from their college experience with a greater appreciation for the reflection process, with the ability to give attention to what challenges them and to engage in an intentional process to understand it more deeply. Indeed, in our interviews, many students commented on "thinking differently" since coming to college, underscoring the change that needs to happen in the thinking process for most college-age students. Clearly this change needs to be intentional and guided by educators.

To make this happen, the college's job is to create formal and informal opportunities for reflection that deepen the learning process, ultimately creating both personal habits and a campus culture of critical reflection. Redundancy is necessary because, as with any skill, this type of analysis requires practice; these opportunities must permeate the college experience. Faculty and staff need to consider where and how they encourage critical reflection: What opportunities do students have to reflect? In what ways is that reflection guided, and how is that guidance graduated so that students are challenged to think ever more deeply and independently?

A campus is brimming with opportunities to foster reflection and integration, from dorm rooms and playing fields to study carrels and seminar tables. No matter the context, the first step is to recognize reflection as a central task of our work. Professor Jim Brown speaks for many of us when he frames teaching as fundamentally a task of supporting students to create knowledge themselves rather than simply recounting knowledge they have been given. Teaching, says Brown, "is about trying to stimulate them—trying to ask provocative questions to get them to think about things and to be creative." Biology professor Linda Niedziela does not shy away from reflective opportunities in the sciences by, for instance, prompting her students to examine their beliefs and values regarding stem cell research. "We make a lot of choices as geneticists, 'Do we do stem cell research? Do we genetically engineer children?' We talk about those questions in terms of 'That's an individual choice, is that good for you?', but we go beyond 'Is it good for you?' 'Is it good for where humans are going on the planet overall?' "

Chaplain emeritus Richard McBride summarizes this work succinctly: "The role of the faculty or the mentor is to present those ill-structured problems and to help name the encounter, name what it is you hope people will see. I think one of the primary moral issues for us is deciding what deserves our attention. The faculty, or the mentors, help people notice things that they might not otherwise be seeing. We can't always contribute; sometimes we can just ponder. But even that is worthwhile; that's a part of growth and the educational progress."

Critical reflection can also be integrated at the curricular level with programs built around discovery of self in a larger context. The University of Louisville's Ideas to Action (i2a) program, for instance, has woven instruction on critical thinking into general education courses, majors, and student life. Students practice and receive feedback in these diverse settings, exploring the ways that reflection is effective and adaptable in diverse contexts. As Louisville students near graduation, they undertake a culminating undergraduate experience meant to demonstrate sophisticated critical thinking in a specific context, such as a capstone disciplinary seminar, community-based research, or an internship.

At Elon, critical reflection has been integrated into every student's education by requiring all undergraduates to complete at least two units of the Experiential Learning Requirement, or ELR, in which students must not only complete a certain activity but also must engage in guided reflection about their learning. By mandating at least two ELRs, Elon's faculty and staff aim to help students develop the skills and habits necessary to learn critically and reflectively from experiences after college.

Reflecting on High-Impact Practices

As we noted earlier, high-impact educational practices (Kuh 2008) are a particularly ripe opportunity for transformational learning. As Professor Pam Kiser told us, the rich contexts of these practices offer significant potential for disorientation and reflection: "Students will have these experiences, but what they do with them in their heads is so much up to us—the questions we ask and the ways we expect them to process their perceptions." Kiser continues, "If you're self-aware and there's something troubling about a situation, you're not just going to say, 'Oh this is troubling, I think I'll go have a beer.' Maybe you will have that beer, but you're still going to keep cranking away at that dissonance: 'Why is that making me uncomfortable?' "

Among Kuh's high-impact practices, study abroad is often cited as one of the most powerful contributors to student transformation in college (Lewin 2009), although its outcomes are not uniformly as powerful as individual stories might suggest (Salisbury, An, and Pascarella 2013). For many undergraduates, immersion in an unfamiliar culture and location prompts questions about both the larger world and the particulars of home. Some students begin to consider questions of poverty and privilege only when they witness the dynamics of a foreign context. In recognizing and beginning to critique the social, economic, cultural, and political structures that shape our world and our individual experiences in that world, students begin to see themselves as part of a larger system rather than simply as isolated individuals.

For Stephanie Badavis, who faced mounting frustration with her inability to make sense of and communicate her experience after taking a course in Guatemala, the challenge came with trying to reconcile the differences of what she had experienced and her life upon her return home. Bre Detwiler, in contrast, was struck not by how different the culture in Ghana was, but how similar it was to her own family's culture. She recognized, for example, similarities in family structure, "in how caregiving is distributed. In Ghana a lot of times we would see a grandmother and lots of children. I see that here, too. My grandmother takes care of all the children; my aunt takes care of her grandchildren. And time. Time is just not a big deal in my family; everybody is late all the time. It's the same in Ghana. Everybody is late all the time." Bre's experience in a distant country gave validation to some aspects of who she was and allowed her to see and appreciate her family in a new way.

But just being exposed to these experiences does not guarantee lasting change. Sometimes we assume that what moves us will move others, just because they encounter it. Chaplain McBride points out that some students return from study abroad holding even more closely to their existing views and values. "Some people come back from a Habitat trip and say, 'Thank God, that's not my life!' That is all they see, just, 'My life is much better than that!'" It is when the experience causes students to question what they have never questioned before that they are open to transformation. As McBride observes, "Others come back and say, 'Why is my life as it is?' 'What are the injustices in society that some are burdened in ways that others are not?'"

To engage in the kind of reflection that has the potential to be transformative, students need careful scaffolding as they prepare to study abroad, as they immerse themselves in the new environment, and after they return. To facilitate some of this, Elon modified its study abroad program to require a one-credit preparatory course for all students before they depart. This short course focuses not on the logistical and practical details but rather on the intellectual and emotional aspects of studying abroad, priming students for ongoing reflection and comparative thinking and, we hope, enhancing their readiness for transformative learning. Based on the success of that preparatory course, Elon's study abroad program now is experimenting with a comparable bookend course to support student reflection as they reenter our community.

In our interviews, all of the students who spoke of the transformative nature of study abroad had reflected in a deep, sustained way on the experience. And all of them had been supported in that reflection, often by faculty and staff mentors but sometimes by peers, parents, or others, who listened carefully and probed thoughtfully as the student struggled to make meaning of her time overseas. We distinguish these students from others who spoke passionately about their time abroad, but who could not describe any changes that resulted from this experience. Thomas Moore, in his book, *A Life at Work* (2008), puts this aptly: "To feel something strongly is not the same as to feel it deeply" (88). Critical reflection makes it possible for study abroad, and other high-impact practices, to be an enduring experience for students, traveling with them wherever they go in the future.

Campus Environments

The college's social, physical, and temporal environments also play a significant role in fostering or inhibiting a culture of critical reflection. In chapter 5, we explore in detail transformative learning outside of the classroom, but it merits some attention here. Student activities and programming serve many purposes in college life. If they are intended to contribute to transformative learning in more than a hit-or-miss way, however, opportunities for critical reflection must be deliberately addressed.

The Office of Student Life at Elon University, for instance, provides cocurricular experiences intended to encourage students "to assume responsibility and make a positive difference for themselves, each other and their communities" with the ultimate goal for students "to live rewarding, creative and purposeful lives." Enacting that mission can be both challenging and highly rewarding.

Like Elon, many colleges host Greek life organizations that can, often powerfully, either enhance or hinder student growth and development (Bureau et al. 2011; DeSimone 2010). For Michael Bumbry, joining the Pi Kappa Phi leadership fraternity his sophomore year, just as he was coming out as a gay man, was a life-changing choice. Although, he says, housing and Greek organizations can be hostile environments for members of the LGBT community, his fraternity brothers welcomed him, even though there were what he calls some "teachable moments" during his time in the fraternity. "There wasn't necessarily a stigma or a homophobic feeling in the chapter, but it was certainly heterosexist. When I say 'heterosexist' I mean automatically assuming that someone is heterosexual, or that you are going to bring a female to social events. So then you come into issues of gender identity and gender expression, gender roles. Not just sexuality, but 'what does being a man actually mean?' You're getting into masculinity—defining men—and then on top of that, another layer defining 'fraternity man.'" In conversation as well as in behavior, Michael sought to educate his fraternity brothers, "pushing it and challenging it just a bit, to have people maybe reconsider their preconceived notions about a particular group of people." As a result, Michael recalls, "they transformed and I transformed."

The physical aspects of a campus also communicate values and support or restrict transformative learning. As Torin Monahan argues, every campus has a "built pedagogy" (2002). Certain activities are more or less probable depending on the design of space and facilities. Are all classrooms essentially alike, or does form follow function? Are study spaces made for solo or collaborative work? Does the layout of offices, buildings, and sidewalks encourage students (and faculty and staff) to encounter people in different disciplines and roles? While the answers to questions like these will vary, Nancy Van Note Chism persuasively notes: "If campuses exist to foster specific kinds of learning, they should inspire and foster this work physically as well as intellectually" (2006, 2.2).

While the design and use of campus space is complex and potentially expensive, creative possibilities exist even on a limited budget. In 2010, for example, Texas Wesleyan University conducted a design competition for students, faculty, and staff to create ClassroomNEXT (Collier, Watson, and Ozuna 2011). Five teams submitted proposals, and the winning design, titled "A Radically-Flexible Classroom," was created by one faculty and five students. The new space is particularly well suited to inquiry-based pedagogies, emphasizing student collaboration in a bright, open room. The ClassroomNEXT program, not surprisingly, inspired changes beyond a single room, as students, faculty, and staff began to re-imagine how spaces across campus could be reconfigured to promote learning and creative engagement.

Stanford University design scholars Scott Doorley and Scott Witthoft remind us that "space transmits culture" (2012, 22). A campus that values transformative learning should reflect that insight—this is a place that is open to change, that allows students to experiment, and that encourages collaboration.

Making Transformation Visible

A strong culture of critical reflection can be communicated overtly and symbolically throughout the university, not only in the physical spaces but also in the curriculum. While the college cannot guarantee transformation among its students—it is highly personal and individualized—we can create a rich environment for transformation by threading opportunities for critical reflection throughout the student's college experience, and by doing all we can to make transformation a visible and valued norm. This is so important because changes in students' self-awareness may be subtle. Professor Pam Kiser notes, "Are you going to look at that person and know that they are transformed? Probably not." But the effect can be profound, especially when it is followed up by other similar opportunities to continue the examination process.

In her education classes, Sarah Gould found that her attitudes about becoming a teacher changed gradually over time, beginning with courses she took her first year. In her sophomore year, her class read a provocative firsthand account of a teacher's experience in a Title I school. "After reading that, our class was pretty much divided in terms of, 'This book made me want to teach in that kind of school' and 'This book scared me.' I was still on the side of, 'This book scared me.' Part of me felt, 'Oh, it's so inspiring! I would love to be one of those teachers that you see in TV movies who go into these horrible school situations and all of the sudden do these fantastic things,' but that's so scary, I don't think that would happen. I don't think I could be that type of teacher."

But in her junior year, in a course on teaching diverse learners, "We talked about the issue of diversity in the classroom: race, gender, religion, learning disability. It was that class that really opened my eyes to the whole issue related to Title I schools . . . and why these students are not succeeding. I think it was that class that not only gave me more of the facts but also gave me the confidence within myself to say, 'Okay, this is something that I do want to do, and I do think I could do it well.'"

Christine Walton, the student who worked with Elon Academy students and wrote a reflection piece for Deborah Long, spoke in her interview about a profound shift in her awareness. She may have had difficulty giving it words, but the reality of it was no less powerful. "I was really involved in a lot of charity-type services, mission projects, and things like that in my freshman and sophomore years. I kind of did them, not as time fillers, I mean, I really did care—I really did care about the purpose behind them, but now I feel like, I don't even know how to describe it, but I just feel like I have this renewed sense of service. It came through working with Elon Academy." She describes her earlier activities as working on real but surface-level issues, unlike her new attention to efforts aimed at addressing the root causes of social ills. Christine attributes this to reflecting on her experiences with low-income students in the Elon Academy. However, in her interview she also tells the story of class readings and discussions in an education course preceding her Elon Academy involvement that made her angry and frustrated with the inequities in educational opportunity in this country. Her coursework primed her to be transformed by the powerful experiences she later had, but she (and others) only noticed this after the fact. Her transformation might seem to have emerged suddenly during one summer, but the roots of change had been growing for at least two years under the surface.

Like Christine, people typically do not recognize transformation while they are in the grips of its intensity; they can only see it clearly after the fact. Purposefully engaging in retrospection helps solidify awareness of the process while also reinforcing the value of that often difficult and trying journey. This looking back allows us to articulate the changes that have occurred and, possibly, to identify the patterns of process that got us there (Parks 2011). Perceiving and appreciating the degree of growth students have undergone is a powerful experience for everyone involved—faculty, staff, parents, peers, and the students themselves. This public reflection also creates exemplars for other students who can see that some of their peers have changed in meaningful ways. Although each student's path might be different, the presence of role models and the expectation of transformation can not only make students more ready and open but also help them navigate the difficulties they will experience along the way.

Loren Pope concludes in *Colleges That Change Lives* (Pope and Oswald 2012) that some schools are better than most in supporting student transformation. These colleges facilitate this awareness and enhance the culture of transformation by finding and creating ways for students to tell their stories. At the City University of New York's Macaulay Honor's College, for instance, students develop portfolios throughout their four years that focus on and chronicle their academic transformation (Light, Chen, and Ittelson 2012, 128). At Augustana College, before graduating students complete a Senior Inquiry course that prompts them to reflect publicly on their learning during college, requiring students both to present their project and to reflect on its implications: "Why did I do this project? What difference does it make? Why might this matter? How does this project fit into my story? Why do I care about this? Who was I when I came to Augustana, and who am I now?" (Henscheid 2012, 105).

Whatever the format, these public reflections can be a powerful way to simultaneously set expectations that such change is important, to reassure everyone that the rocky process is normal, and to express the community's shared commitment to student transformation.

Barriers to a Culture of Critical Reflection

As institutions of higher education strive for educational excellence in a rapidly changing environment with diminishing budgets and new online rivals appearing, faculty and staff often find themselves struggling to juggle their many responsibilities. As the number of initiatives and committees directed at change and improvement grow, so do the tasks and time-consuming obligations of the faculty and staff. This culture of busy-ness can work, both practically and perceptually, against practices of critical reflection.

For faculty to promote reflection among their students, they must be able to engage in it themselves. Moore (2009) recommends an attitude of contemplation in the workplace. "Contemplation is . . . a quieting of inner and outer activity. It produces calm and allows some relief from the frenetic activity of ordinary life and from the incessant thoughts connected to various anxieties" (166). He advocates a soulful life at work. "That means living from a deep place and taking the time to tend to your family, your home, and your friendships. It means being a real person on the job and being connected to the work you do. . . . A soulful life is one of thoughtfulness, care, and engagement—you are present in everything you do, not just going through the motions" (103). As faculty dash from class to office hours to committee meetings and then home to more responsibilities, a contemplative orientation toward work can seem alien or even, sadly, laughable. Still, if we truly value this capacity in our students, we surely need to be able to model it for them—at least sometimes (Felten et al. 2013).

For students, one of the ubiquitous barriers to reflective analysis is the "checklist" mentality of many of today's college students, particularly the goal-driven, high-achieving ones. Beginning in middle school, students are presented with lists of courses they need to fulfill college requirements. And some of their parents may have been cultivating this checklist since preschool! In high school, there is a college prep list and a list beyond that to be really competitive for college. Extracurricular and volunteer activities are often chosen with an eye toward which will best fill the blanks on a college application.

Once in college, students find the checklist even more important. What courses are needed to fill major requirements? What needs to be done to get an A? What do they need to do to get a good shot at an internship, an interview, and eventually a job? The checklists seem to continue. There's even a "bucket list"—a checklist to accomplish before you kick the bucket! "Time management" often means figuring out how to get the most tasks accomplished in the shortest amount of time.

The Checklist Manifesto by Atul Gawande (2009) lifts the checklist to new heights as it advocates for a systematic approach to accomplishing important goals. But Gawande's checklist approach grew out of his experience in the world of medical and surgical practice where preventing mistakes and increasing efficiency are paramount, often a matter of life and death. Transformative learning is different. It is not about getting the A in the quickest and most painless way. It is about allowing, even embracing, mistakes. It is about exploring and considering possibilities. It is about going deep, a task that is neither easily defined nor readily confined to a checklist.

In *The Art of Possibility* (2002), Benjamin and Rosamund Zander explore an experiment in "giving an A." Students are promised an A in an intense orchestra class, but to receive it, each student must write a letter to the professor at the beginning of the course. The letter, dated at the end of the semester, tells the professor why students deserve an A, projecting the changes they hope to undergo as an outcome of the class. The examples are powerful, as students look past getting an A and get on with the task of fulfilling their big dreams, of becoming who they want to be.

The problem with a checklist approach is that it does not create an openness to new views. The focus is on achieving closure on one thing in order to move to the next. With such future orientation, little attention is available for the present. Task orientation leaves scant room for the vagaries of reflection. But in transformation, the process is inextricable from the product, and going deep makes going forward perhaps a bit less rapid. A checklist approach in itself is not bad, but when the ultimate goal becomes accomplishing a task rather than achieving a greater purpose—for example, becoming a doctor rather than healing people—it can derail the process of transformation. Students may not even realize there is some-thing beyond a checklist, certainly not an option that would be equally desirable. Their checklists have served them well, even gotten them into the college they are currently attending, and earned them some As. So it requires particular attention on the part of faculty and staff to encourage the more ambiguous process of reflection.

For the learner, the emotional element of the critical reflection process can also present a significant barrier. Unlike the checklist approach to col-lege (and to life in general), which can be comforting as it offers the prom-ise of control and predictability, the adventure of transformation is rife with discomfort, ambiguity, and surprises. When Rainey Bezila was asked what she thought transformation meant, she replied, "I think it means get-ting closer to your fullest potential. And not necessarily knowing what that looks like exactly." While it can seem counterintuitive that at an institution of higher education, we are promoting the value of not knowing, this stance creates an essential openness to what can be learned through reflective analysis.

The strong emotions that often accompany the process of reflective analysis are also a rich source for examination (Chickering and Reissner 1993). Frustration, for example, is a common response to the dismantling of long-held beliefs and values or perspectives. It is natural to try to avoid or minimize uncomfortable or "negative" emotions, but feelings such as frustration and anger can provide valuable motivation and momentum for change. Learning to sit with these feelings, exploring and reflecting on them—even welcoming them—can deepen the analysis process. An emo-tional response *is* a response and can be an integral part of the reflective process. When students learn not just to tolerate these emotions but even to watch for them and to accept them as indications of growth, they have learned a valuable life lesson: valuing the emotional element rather than just experiencing it.

To some degree, pain and loss are inherent in the transformative process (Boyd and Myers 1988; Scott 1997). As Amy Rittenour recounts, "There have been courses that have really challenged everything that I've known. . . . Those experiences that really make you totally reexamine where you've been coming from for the past nineteen years of your life are some of the hard-est moments."

Awareness that loss goes with transformation can help learners hang on during the confusion and emotional upheaval that they will experience. If they know it is a normal part of the process, they may be able to tolerate it better. This perspective imparts the courage to keep going; and students may more quickly recognize the process when it shows up later in their lives, giving them a better chance of transferring their transformative learning skills to life beyond college. Larissa Ferretti learned to recognize and appreciate the emotional aspect of transformative learning and to transfer it to other situations, "because I've felt that discomfort before," she says, "and I know it ends up putting me in a really great place. With Guatemala I cried when I left my dad at the airport. But, when I was coming back, I was crying because I didn't want to leave Guatemala. I've felt that feeling before so I know, 'This is going to be okay, you're doing the right thing.' Even though it doesn't feel right, it's the right kind of wrong."

Questioning Identity

As students dismantle what they have known, they often find themselves questioning their very identity. Students reflect not only on what they are doing or feeling in an experience, but on who they are. The goal of critical reflection is twofold: first to allow students to move forward in meaningful transformation during the college period. The second, related aim is for students to own the reflective process, integrating it into their lives and applying it to other aspects of their identity. As Larissa told us during her senior year, "I think I still don't really know exactly who I am. I'm becoming okay with that, I guess, and becoming okay with the idea that it's a constant learning process."

As with all of transformative learning, we cannot predict how critical reflection will manifest itself in the lives of students. For Amy, it took the form of a tattoo. "I took an anthropology course my freshman year that really shaped a lot of my views about things," says Amy. She went on:

One of the last chapters we covered was about body art and tattooing. I've always felt things like "That is so gross; bikers get tattoos and that is so disgusting." But we learned why it's done and how it's done across so many different cultures. It's supposed to represent a major turning point in your life, a physical reminder of what you've achieved and what you've done and the point you were at when you got it. . . . Then I got to London and I realized, this is my transformative moment. I know this is where I want to come back to and this is what I want to do with my life. It was just one of those moments. So I went and got a tattoo. It's just a little thing, a North Star, on my ankle, but every time I see that, it's like a part of London with me. It's like a promise to myself that I'm going to be back there and I'm going to be doing what I want to do, because I know I can do it now.

Chris Manor's experience illustrates this shift in educational responsibility well.

I grew up thinking what I assumed every other student thought and the majority of students still think: What do I want to get out of this class? An A. The thought of actively trying to learn something never crossed my mind. Then one day as we were discussing this chapter, we happened upon the subject of teacher and student responsibility and then *Wham!* the realization hit me: What were my own responsibilities for my education? It was such an odd question. Why had I not thought of this before? The more I thought about it, the more it shook everything I associated with education and learning—how I had done homework, written papers—everything had been completely turned on end. I had been watching my education pass me by without ever taking part. I struggled with this question (and still do) because I had never been confronted with taking responsibility for my own education. (Manor et al. 2010, 5)

Ben Smith expands this responsibility beyond the classroom:

I think my experiences have made me more receptive and more aware of the role I play as a global citizen, what my role is as a person in this world. I think these experiences, definitely what they've done, they've defined—I have come to see where I fit in the whole grand scheme of things, where my experiences have placed me and what kind of experiences I have and what I have to offer. They've made me realize what responsibility that gives me as a member of a community, as a citizen of the country, as a global citizen.

From Reflection to Action

Transformation is about making a connection to something larger, something beyond ourselves. As students take responsibility for their own reflective processes, they also begin to take ownership of their identities and responsibility for their place in the larger community. To increase the likelihood that the intense experiences we design for our students will yield the kind of transformations we are hoping for, the reflective process cannot be left to chance. Reflection needs to be intentional, built in, guided, and critical; practice builds infrastructure that fosters such reflection, and infrastructure is important for lifelong skills. As critical reflection makes students aware of expanded possibilities for looking at and living in the world around them, it prepares them to take action.

CHAPTER FOUR

Moved to Action

"Even at the end of that bike ride, I still couldn't believe I'd done it. I think we all have experiences where we wake up and say, 'Oh, that changed my life,' then realize three days later, it didn't. It changed your thinking for a short time, but it didn't change what you do. I think the ultimate test of Journey of Hope changing my life is that I still think about it, and I still do things differently because of it."

Brian O'Shea spent the summer after his junior year bicycling across the country with seventy-five other men from his national collegiate fraternity as a part of a fundraiser called Journey for Hope that benefitted people with disabilities. It wasn't an action he came to easily. "It was something I had thought about a lot but, knowing myself, probably wasn't going to do. I thought, 'You know, that really fits with who I am and what I want to do, but I just can't see myself cycling across the country.'"

Eventually, however, Brian did send in his application for Journey of Hope and was accepted. "It didn't feel real until I got to San Francisco and started training with men there. It still makes me sort of tear up to read that first journal entry. I was terrified. I can still see myself sitting on that bunk bed, thinking and writing. Terrified that I was about to cycle 100 miles the next day. I couldn't even think about the whole summer, just the next day alone. . . . But I did it. I did it for sixty-three days."

Brian recalls: "It was the hardest work of my life, the hardest on my body I've ever put myself through." The cross-country ride challenged more than Brian's physical stamina, however. His experience fundraising and working with people with disabilities across the country also changed the way he thought about, spoke about, and interacted with people with disabilities. "I realized that I'm capable of things larger than I thought.'"

Reflection and analysis, when performed with diligence, lead students to an awareness of their own place in a larger world, an understanding that they have choices in how they live their lives and that those choices affect others. It leads to an awareness of the responsibility to take action in response to a new understanding or a new commitment. Thus to be transformative, reflective awareness must be followed up with verification—action that clarifies and confirms this new way of being. Verification is about answering the questions, "What is it I want or need to become and what actions does that require?" "What do I need to enact?" The verification part of the process has students trying those new ways on, seeing what fits and what does not and what feels true and what does not, and acting out their new understandings in the community around them. These actions provide vital confirmation of this new state. As Sharon Parks (2011) stresses, if there is a change, a true deep change, it will be evident in the behaviors that emanate from it.

We have all seen students who appear to be moved by experiences but who are not actually moved to action, whose internal changes never make it to external manifestation. As one student mentioned to one of us after a particularly intense classroom debate, "All of this talk of poverty makes me depressed. I need to go buy a new purse to feel better." While that might be an acceptable coping mechanism for some students, it is not a sign of transformation. Designing experiences to encourage students to follow through with actions increases the likelihood of real, long-term change.

Action yields feedback for the student. Actions create consequences, and those consequences allow the student to evaluate the actions' alignment with their new beliefs. Christine Walton, for example, was well on her way to graduating from Elon with a major in communications, but her work with the Elon Academy let her see that that major wasn't the right match for her. "My sophomore year I was realizing I didn't want to do what I was doing anymore. I didn't want to work in media. I didn't want to work with public relations. . . . I thought that was what I wanted to do, but that wasn't for me. My passions were for education and being with kids. I looked at my resume, and all of my extracurricular activities were volunteering at an elementary school, doing camps, babysitting. My communications professor was saying I needed to have an internship at a newspaper, but I realized I wanted to go into teaching." So, despite having accumulated credits toward one major, Christine changed paths and began work as a human service studies major because that fit with who she had become.

Bre Detwiler also changed her major after her experiences in the classroom and experiential learning activities helped her better understand who she was: "I came in with a totally different thought for my future. . . . Then I got into environmental studies. I got so interested in community issues here in Alamance County, it made everything blow up for me and it clicked. There was kind of an 'Aha!' moment about my sophomore year: 'This is what you should do; you're supposed to do *this* for the rest of your life.' "

Identity and Action

Stories of transformation ultimately deal with self-identity, and actions provide clarification about one's identity. Brian O'Shea's eventual participation in Journey of Hope, for example, reconciled his sense of who he was—a service-oriented man with a heart for others—with his actions, taking him from "that really fits with who I am and what I want to do, but I just can't see myself cycling across the country" to "I did it!" and "it changed my life." For Olivia Hubert-Allen, a study abroad experience in London produced a significant change in how she viewed herself, one that took time to be fully integrated.

In my internship, I worked in the press office at the Liberal Democrats, which is the third political party there, doing media relations stuff. Being in a field that was also really competitive and kind of snappy, it made me—I hate to say "more selfish," but it sort of did. It woke me up. I felt like before I went abroad and before I had this internship, I was really passive and willing to do anything for anybody. That was just the person who I was; I was this giver. I came back and thought, "You know what? This is my life, and I'm going to have to start not just giving, but deciding what I want and taking as well, just having my direction and my own independence." I think that's what I mean when I say I wasn't sure if I liked it because I came back a more selfish person than when I went over. Now a year removed, I've found a good balance between the two. I'm not this awful selfish person. I'm not a person who is afraid to get what she needs and what she wants, either.

For some students, a struggle with sexual identity features prominently in their college experiences. Michael Bumbry was one such student. "Freshman year, I dealt with a lot of identity issues. When talking about transformation, the paramount one for me was sexual identity. I came out as a gay male around fall break time. I had a team of supportive peers who had no issues or problems, certainly at least any that were known. That doesn't always happen on college campuses. LGBT people are typically isolated and feel alienated, especially in residence halls. So to have that support network at 17, my first semester in college when I was still figuring out so many other things, not just sexual orientation but also just adjusting was very important." As so often happens, the confidence Michael gained through his actions and the support of his peers spilled over into other areas, promoting his continued growth throughout college. "The service learning community was absolutely instrumental in my ability to develop, but it was also having the confidence to move into the other areas of the university that I ultimately ended up pursuing."

University faculty and staff often witness pieces of this process. For instance, biology professor Linda Niedziela describes the changes she witnessed in one of her students, not what she would label a transformation as such, but a student in the *process* of transformation, and of verification in particular, seeing herself as a scientist and growing in the confidence of that:

Lab for us is normally the time you see personalities come out. In her first year, one of my students was intense but still very quiet. Then her second year, she was in my sophomore seminar course, which is a course that teaches scientific writing and communication. It was the students' first time to do some real independent research. What I saw was that it really turned her on. It was a switch from being that student who sat in class and loved learning but didn't take that step to being the one to discuss things or to initiate conversations. She was really excited about the research project, so I invited her to take a research lab with me. . . .

That really opened a door for her. She became more confident in her own ability to learn and to find answers to her own questions. In the research lab, she realized, "I can go out and find the answer to that question, or I can come up with a question of my own and investigate it."

"As time went on," Niedzela says, "when she took an upper level class with me . . . I saw a complete difference in personality. Her ability to take a project and ask a question—ask a really deep question—was way beyond her classmates. She had confidence in her own ability to learn. She went from, 'Whatever Dr. N says, I'll learn that and that's fine,' to actually being able to question me. If I said something she didn't think was quite right she would challenge me, especially in the research lab. She's currently at Vanderbilt getting her PhD in pharmacology and loving it, absolutely loving the opportunity to investigate things and look really deep."

Actions also anchor internal changes. For Stephanie Badavis, choosing not to be in a sorority marked the internal changes that began to take place during her all-important Guatemala experience.

I joined a sorority my freshman year, and I kind of liked it. . . . I was in the middle of figuring out whether I wanted to continue with it or not when I went to Guatemala. I saw extreme poverty there, and I remember calling my mom and saying, "I don't want this." It's a lot of money being in a sorority. Seeing that poverty and knowing that that money could go somewhere else, realizing that being in a sorority or being with that group of girls just was not me. It was just a step to being able to realize that I can separate myself from that and be comfortable with it. I would say that study abroad changed my life. I studied abroad in Guatemala my sophomore year, I studied abroad in Spain for a semester in the fall of my junior year, and I'm going to South Africa this year as a senior. I think traveling to different places is a way to be self-aware and to look at your prejudices and realize that you want to break out of those and become more culturally confident, to become just an overall better person.

Deciding to act is a commitment to change, a commitment to respond to more than a transient emotion, to live out the results of one's reflection and analysis. An action captures the energy of an experience in a form that can be maneuvered, repeated, and modified. Even seemingly profound experiences will fade if not acted upon. The action allows us to name the change, bring it to a higher level of consciousness and workability, and embed it in daily life.

Sometimes an action may look no different on the outside but still represent a significant internal change. The process of reflection and analysis does not always result in relinquishing previous behaviors. Sometimes it is a matter of understanding old actions within a new framework. The action may be small or appear even to be unchanged, but the thoughts and intentions supporting those choices have changed: the context in which the learner sees it is significantly different. For instance, one student customarily walked from her off-campus apartment to class because she enjoyed the views along the way, but after a powerful course on environmental sustainability she understood the value of walking instead of driving as an act of stewardship for the earth. Someone observing this student walking to class would not be able to perceive a change in that moment; but because the action is anchoring a much deeper awareness and commitment, that internal shift will almost certainly manifest itself visibly in her life years down the road.

Bre Detwiler's continued visits to NASCAR races are another example of action that belies an internal change. "I'm a big environmentalist now," she says, "and I still love NASCAR. I can't give it up! I understand it pollutes, but I love it. I love everything about NASCAR. . . . NASCAR to me is family, it's a family thing. My dad does it, and my sisters do it. For me it's like a cultural tradition, and I'm okay with that. I'm just going to work toward making NASCAR greener. I'm going to encourage things like the changing of fuels. They're moving their fuels over to unleaded because they were leaded, and that's not very good for people at the track. I am going to encourage those good things."

Similarly, it would be no surprise to people who knew Sarah Gould in her pre-college years that she planned to vote in the upcoming presidential election. But for Sarah herself, the action represents a new sense of agency and responsibility, grounded in her developed view of herself and her place in the world. "I think probably the biggest change in my underlying beliefs is the concept of actually having an impact on other people," Sarah says, continuing:

I was always raised that it's important to vote and to share your opinion, but I don't think I ever realized how important that was until I started being really interested and involved in the issues that underlie why I made the decisions I made. For example, I've been following the political campaigns really intently. A huge part of that is because, first of all, this is the first presidential election I can vote in. That's very empowering. But now it will directly impact my life and career; any educational policies and decisions that are made will affect me and therefore the students I teach. I feel like if I want to have an impact, I need to do what is my responsibility to do and participate in that way.

How Sarah acts has not necessarily changed, but how she *thinks* of that act is going to steer her life beyond this election and beyond Elon. For many learners, a lot may be going on beneath the surface that is invisible to the observer, but the actions, especially initially, demonstrate to the individual that a change has taken place. Intentionality is connected to the action, even if that action initially looks no different to an outside observer; the change has anchored forward movement in the transformative journey.

Acting in Public

When looking for evidence of change in students, colleges and universities often make the mistake of focusing on engagement and of assuming that change is happening as a result. Engagement in high-impact practices (Kuh 2008), as we have seen, is a necessary but early step in the transformative process. Universities must beware of making assumptions about the presence or absence of transformation underlying particular behaviors. For example, to measure global citizenship among their students, some colleges count the number of students who have passports. But having a passport does not in and of itself represent a commitment to global citizenry. Perhaps the student was taken on a cruise with his parents in high school, or she wants to spend part of her summer overseas where the legal drinking age is lower. It's not the presence of a passport that signals transformation but rather what will be done with the passport.

Spiritual teacher and scholar Eknath Easwaran, in his book *Words to Live By* (2010), talks about two kinds of travel—horizontal and vertical.

Horizontal travel refers to moving from one place to another, as we do when we visit a foreign country. It is exciting, it feels different; *you* feel different because you are you in a different place. But if that is the only "traveling" you do, the changes will wear off once you return home to your familiar surroundings. Easwaran suggests there is immense value to be found in *vertical* travel, in which we look inward, using the situation we are in to examine ourselves and our place in the world.

Within the college experience, we tend to emphasize study abroad in a horizontal travel sense, establishing programs and counting the percentage of students who travel abroad before graduating. But without the accompanying vertical travel, it may all be effort and money spent for window dressing only. It is the vertical travel that results in change, evident in the fact that college students can be deeply engaged in changing the welfare of the world at their own backdoor, no passport needed.

Behaviors emerging as a result of a well-examined life, even if they do not appear different at first, are likely to lead to significant visible changes later on, beyond the college years. Ultimately, therefore, actions, when looked at closely and carefully, do serve as indicators to oneself and to the community. Not only do the students see themselves as having a new or enhanced identity, but, as their actions build, others begin seeing them that way, too. We might say that personal transformation is not complete until it is acted upon in the larger community, until it has affected others.

History professor Jim Brown expresses concern, however, about how often this awareness actually translates into action. He describes his experiences teaching the "Global Experience" courses required for all Elon students in which they are exposed to many harsh realities of the world.

> The problem for them is they realize the world isn't the way they thought it was. That's the dissonance. They are suddenly seeing things that affect millions of people, and they had no idea about it. . . . Most of them come from backgrounds that are very comfortable. Then they realize other people are out there who aren't comfortable. . . . I always wonder after the last day of exams what happens. I go through a class that's moving, for me, and then they get up, and immediately, on their way out, they're talking about where they're going to go to lunch.

Professor Brown continues, "A more extreme example is the World War II study abroad course. We go to Auschwitz, and they come back and write in their journals how this has changed their outlook on life, how they look at the world in a different way. I'm pretty cynical about that. I want to come back in six months and say, 'What's up with that?' . . . You need to bring that back. You need to *do* something and make it worthwhile, or else it was just a tour."

But, as we found in our interviews, some students do make lasting changes. As Christine Walton says of her experiences putting her renewed passion for education into practice, "I had experiences when I went abroad for a semester in Spain, being able to teach, being able to tutor English over there. Seeing how different learning processes work and how I function as a teacher and then putting that directly into practice in the Elon Academy was amazing. . . . Changing their entire lives changed my life. That really affected what I want to do with my life; it's impacted my decisions about where I'm going to work in the world. Whatever I do, I know that it's going to be in service to others."

Overcoming Barriers to Action

The question is this: how do we make these follow-through actions more common and more the norm for our college students and graduates? To answer it, we must consider what it is that prevents students from taking such action, what makes them "immune to change" (Kegan and Lahey 2009). Certainly students need opportunities to put their new ideas into practice. The timing of those activities, however, may be just as important. Let's look again at Jim Brown's Global course, a course commonly credited with student awakenings. The course creates dissonance for students by exposing them to challenging realities. There is follow up with reflection and dialogue that students often find moving, and the course concludes with a call to action. "We talk about the necessity for action: 'What do *you* do about this?'" Professor Brown asks his students. "For the final project in the class, the student picks a nongovernmental organization and talks not just about giving money but other ways they could get involved with that NGO right now."

We spoke with a student from that class who was disturbed to learn that human trafficking occurs even in the United States. She acknowledged that she learned things she could do in response to that through the course. "Have you done anything?" we asked. "I haven't, unfortunately," she replied candidly. "I guess right now, I'm not—I guess maybe when I get a job and I'm financially well off, I could do more. Right now I'm a college kid, so . . ."

Perhaps this reluctance to respond should not surprise us. It could be that at this developmental stage, students simply do not see themselves as actors in the world. Jeffrey Arnett, author of *Emerging Adulthood*, suggests that young people in their early twenties who are not committing, be it to relationships, home ownership, or possibly even behavioral changes related to their understanding of the world, are simply acting their age. He suggests there is a "changing timetable for adulthood," allowing today's emerging adults to delay verification—the process of confirming a new belief structure through trial and error—in an extended period of experimentation and in-betweenness. But perhaps, as this student continues her development, if she encounters similar situations with clear avenues for action as she approaches her senior year, she may be more inclined to weave those changes into her current life.

Students are also often overwhelmed by the magnitude of the problems they encounter. Professor Tom Arcaro describes an example from an academic program's AIDS education project in Namibia:

> After we came back with that first documentary video footage from Namibia, students were feeling that, "Oh my God, there are real people over there, and there are some real, desperate problems." We came back with interviews with families with AIDS, child-headed households. We interviewed a 15-year-old who's the head of a household with two younger sisters and a younger brother. How do you respond to that on an emotional level? Then multiply that case by the thousands of cases we found there. So the students get to this emotional overload level. They responded with things like, "I can't deal with this anymore, I just want to go to West End and have a beer because this is just too big."

It can be hard to imagine that any single action a lone college student is capable of taking could make a significant dent in a problem of such magnitude. Helping students develop ways to process their emotions, and then helping them understand how they can act on the problem, alone and in community, can move them past this hurdle (Loeb 1999).

Verification requires a willingness to take a zigzagging path as students step out into action. Students who strive for simple "checklist" success and who are strangers to failure can be reluctant to risk the "error" inherent in trial and error. They may need overt permission, even encouragement, to take risks, to stretch themselves and not worry about making mistakes and positive acknowledgement when they do step beyond their comfort zones even though they may not reach their goals. Guidance in examining their failures and the lessons and meanings those experiences hold for them can actually increase their resilience—and their ultimate ability to succeed.

As a recent graduate, Michael Bumbry reflected on the role of these sorts of failures in the transformative process:

> I think there does need to be some conscious, intentional thought on the part of the college: "What do we want our students to get out of the 'blank' experience—the Elon experience, the Duke experience?" . . . Allowing students to stumble, to fall, to bump up a bit, to maybe mess up and start from scratch, kind of mess up along the way. Then, hopefully between the broad areas that the university has set—"These are the values, this is what we hope you will gain"—and the kind of trial and error that the student goes through, at the end of the day, hopefully there's transformation.

Institutional Support for Verification

According to engagement theory (Kuh 2003), two essential factors contribute to student learning and development in college: what the students do and what the institution does to support student action. Where are the chances within the college years for students to act out their values? Are frequent opportunities available to all students or only to a select few? Are these experiences threaded throughout all four years?

All skill development—including, for instance, the skills of being global citizens, inspired leaders, or other manifestations of college values—

takes practice. It is therefore important for the university to create opportunities for students to practice those skills that we hope will become lifelong capacities—to attempt difficult things, get meaningful feedback, and respond with appropriate actions.

The University of Notre Dame has a variety of programs designed to support verification and to assist students in navigating the tensions they will face while balancing desires for personal achievement and social change. For instance, at graduation many students wear ribbons to publicly affirm a pledge to "investigate and take into account the social and environmental consequences of any job [they] consider, thereby striving to create a just, peaceful, and nonviolent world" (Colby et al. 2003, 68).

At the University of Illinois in Urbana-Champaign students created a format for sharing their commitment to act. After the devastating earthquake in Haiti in 2010, students at the university, like their peers across the country and around the world, mobilized to raise funds for relief efforts and to supply aid to the victims. As students and the local community worked together over a weekend to pack a million meals for shipment to Haiti, students lined one wall with butcher paper and asked people to write about what motivated them to act. Hundreds of students, and many faculty, staff, and community members, created a public testament to their individual and shared commitment to enact their values in a time of tragedy (Patel 2012, 122–23).

This attention to acting in the face of difficulty and even disaster, to managing goals that may conflict, is essential for helping students to transform on our campuses and to remain open to transformative learning in the future. Elon's Professor Kiser remembers a student who struggled with this after a winter term abroad:

> She had a major shift in worldview; she came back feeling as though her whole life had been wrapped up in a lot of superficial, materialistic things that didn't matter. . . . She was in a sorority, and she talked about coming back to Elon right after winter term when sorority rush was going on. . . . The thing that I remember about her was that she was having trouble sustaining the transformation. She was having trouble figuring out, "I feel like I see what life is about, and *I don't know what to do with that now.*" She used a metaphor that was so telling. She said, "I feel

like all my life I've been on this game board, and I've been moving pieces on that game board. I went away, and I was with people who were on an entirely different game board. Their game board was getting through the day, having enough food and water, loving their families, this very simple game board. . . . Now I'm back and I feel like I've got to get on my old game board, but I don't like that game board."

Kiser suggests "that may be a neglected part of this transformation process. As students have these really powerful insights, what do they do with them and how do they sustain them? What can we as faculty and as an educational institution do to help students with that transition? I would be curious to know what has happened to her now. That was winter term her senior year, and I taught her in the spring. I just wonder what she did with that. We always talk about transformation as having a positive valence, and it does, but then there is a difficult side, too. That 'so what?' question. 'What does this mean for me, my future, how I spend my time, how I spend my money, what I do with my life?'" The institution that creates challenging and inspiring experiences for its students must also make a place for "changed" students to re-engage, to plug back in, and to move forward.

Mentoring can improve students' abilities to be successful in this thorny process (Johnson 2006; Zachary 2011). Professor Kiser says of mentoring, "It's not that I don't think transformation can happen without us, but I think you get a bigger bang for your buck if there is somebody, a person who is further along in the journey—I don't know that it has to be a faculty member—there facilitating that."

Sarah Gould, for example, simply needed someone to show her that it could be done. She had become interested in meeting the educational needs of the most disadvantaged students by teaching in Title I schools. She recognized the problem of educational inequality and was angry that so few people were doing anything about it, but she was still unsure about moving forward herself. It took encountering role models to tip her into action. She recalls,

I thought, "Okay, I could do this. I could do this. Maybe. I don't know." That's when the nervousness and the lack of confidence took over. Then we had visiting teachers come in from a very successful Title I school not far away. They came and talked to us. As I was sitting there, I was thinking, "Okay, they're doing it; it's not impossible. It's not that if I went into this situation, after two months of teaching I would want to quit and leave the profession," which I think is the stereotype of teachers who venture into that situation. I think then I got to the point of, "Okay, I can *do* this; now I *want* to do this."

Initially the guidance may be heavily directive. For example, a student must complete a certain number of experiences to fulfill the mandated Experiential Learning Requirement or complete the work needed to earn credit for an undergraduate research project. Such required experiences have pushed many students to take steps they otherwise would not have taken and have built their confidence and enthusiasm in the process. As students are capable of noticing, questioning, thinking, and acting for themselves, however, the mentoring can become less directive.

To achieve this goal, faculty at the University of Michigan and Eastern Michigan University have adapted *hevruta* as a technique to move students away from depending on professors and toward using peers as their primary source of insight into disciplinary material. *Hevruta* is a sustained conversational pairing that is common in yeshivas, Jewish schools that focus on religious education. In a yeshiva, a *hevruta* might persist for years, while in an academic course it typically is constrained to a single, intense semester. In his upper-level English course, for instance, Professor Ralph Williams adapted *hevruta* because, although he tried many different pedagogies over the years, "Often, genuine discussion doesn't occur at all. The teacher becomes the focus of all questions, and the session turns into a catechetical question-and-answer session" (quoted in Wright, Bernstein, and Williams 2013, 107). By having students work in a *hevruta* from the first day of class through the end of the term, Williams found that "sustained partnerships could help [students] develop the trusting relationship needed to grapple more deeply with the complexities encountered in a text and with the partner's lived experience" (107).

Professor Jeff Bernstein at Eastern Michigan University has adapted *hevruta* for his political science students, using the semester-long pairs not only to assist students in developing their disciplinary knowledge but also to enhance whole class conversations by helping students gain confidence in their own analysis of the complex material (Wright, Bernstein, and Williams 2013, 117).

Cultivating this kind of intellectual and personal independence is not an easy process; scholars of mentoring sometimes refer to this as the "separation phase" or as "fading" (Allen and Eby 2010). Many students can feel neglected or even abandoned by people they had considered mentors, and the faculty or staff member can feel superfluous. Once again, as with highlighting the intentionality behind actions, making the transformative process—including the role of guides and mentors—explicit helps both the students and the institution's faculty and staff.

Verification beyond Campus

When the infrastructure of the college scaffolds students' opportunities to act on their emerging commitment, it encourages them to take their actions beyond the borders of the university. Jill Medhus, for example, was moved by her college experiences to reach past the programs offered by Elon. She is planning a trip to a developing country to work with an HIV teen clinic. "Actually," Jill says, "that had a lot to do with my experiences in Global, just realizing that there's a huge world and a lot of opportunity beyond my little bubble. I saw it as something I could influence, shape, and mold . . . I thought, 'I could have a huge impact on somebody somewhere in the world, beyond Elon, beyond my home state of New Jersey.'"

Professor Jim Brown, who expressed concern about awareness translating to action, might be somewhat reassured by Jill's story, but how do we make this an even more common behavior for college students? What expectations and encouragements are there for students to extend their actions beyond the existing infrastructure?

Every choice to act is a choice to support a particular paradigm, value, or way of looking at the world. A student's action in support of a new way of thinking, therefore, builds strength for that view. Choosing not to act in support of that view is, in effect, acting contrary to the new way, nipping transformation in the bud—well, in the bloom, perhaps—minimizing the fruit that the internal work bears. The hope is that graduates will continue their commitment to acting on the values and purposes they identified as meaningful during their college years. This sustained effort is facilitated by finding a supportive environment, remaining in contact with people who both support and challenge one's views, and engaging in activities that confirm the value of our efforts.

An unusual but effective example of such a sustained context, consciously built into the structure of the program itself, is the Periclean Scholars program at Elon. Project Pericles, sponsored by the Eugene Lang Foundation, is committed to raising the level of civic engagement and social responsibility of the entire university community. The group of students known as Periclean Scholars work together to identify and achieve a civic goal. A unique characteristic of this college group, however, is that they remain a group after graduation. To sustain their commitment, members of the group continue to stay connected to the larger purpose that originally motivated them, working together on socially directed tasks.

The Center for Civic Engagement and Leadership at St. Lawrence University aims for similar ends with its Community Mentors program. Like comparable organizations on many campuses, the center coordinates academic and cocurricular efforts to develop citizenship skills and capacities in undergraduates. The Community Mentor program is somewhat distinct in its emphasis on student ownership of this mission. Community Mentors are students who serve as paid members of the center's staff, working with community partners to identify assets and problems and then to develop programs to address these needs. By empowering students to take the lead in the center's efforts, the Community Mentor program helps develop students who can be "agents of positive social change both on and off campus" (Flores, Crosby-Currie, and Zimmerman 2007, 11).

This emphasis on students seeing themselves as connected with and capable of contributing positively to a community is a hallmark of transformative learning. As a result of the process, a person commits to a new—or recommits to an existing—purpose. In Jill Medhus's passionate description of her plans for her work with the teen HIV clinic, she comments that she is motivated by a desire "to give back to the community as much as possible." Jill's sense of responsibility and agency grew during her time in college, and she wants to act. However, she is choosing to do that in a community she has never been a part of, "giving back" to somewhere she has never been. It is her new sense of connectedness to a larger world, the fact that she sees it all as part of the same whole, that allows her to think this way. After Brian O'Shea completed his arduous cycling trip across the country, "I realized that I'm capable of things larger than I thought." He plans to do it again as part of his lifelong commitment to working with and advocating for people with disabilities.

It is easy for students to see their four years of college as a discrete block of time in which to act in aberration to regular life, four years apart from the "real world." Transformation is a lifelong process, however, not a four-year gig. Reflecting on her college years, Amy Rittenour concludes: "Sometimes I think you can lose perspective on the fact that, yes, I love Elon, but it's just Elon. There is so much else out there in the world. You can lose perspective on the fact that this is just four years of your life and there's so much more ahead of you, that this is just trying to get you ready for it." Rather than being limiting, "just Elon" in this context means that the university has become the core of a much larger sphere of influence, achieving its ultimate goal.

Giving Back for Life

When students are aware of significant things that need doing and see themselves as people who are capable of doing such things, it is a prime opportunity for moving their passion into a lifetime of purposeful action. Repeated actions become habits. But, even more important, when repeated with intention, they become practices, actions imbued with purpose. A habit is something done repeatedly with the goal of performing the action, whereas a practice is done with a purpose outside the action for its own sake. Habits can maintain a new relationship with the surrounding community, but a practice can take it to another level.

An educational process that makes transformative learning, including the verification process, explicit for the learner increases the likelihood that the transformative journey will continue beyond the college years. We can ask students, and even alumni, "Who or what is it you want to become? What actions would be consistent with that?" We can engage them in explicit dialogues when talking about the college process, with such questions as "What does it mean for you to become a scholar? An artist? An entrepreneur? How would that look different from your life now?" These are conversations that bring students to a higher level of consciousness about the choices they are making to get where they are going, a process that can continue even after graduation. Many universities, including Elon, connect with alumni through a range of programs designed to foster professional development, community, and philanthropy. The opportunity to support alumni, particularly young alumni, in transformative learning beyond college offers great potential to enhance the growth and development students experience while on campus.

Deep, positive, and meaningful change in students engenders a certain type of loyalty to the people and institutions that supported and guided them through that process. When universities ask alumni to "give back," the implication is that the students were given something in the first place, something more than just a diploma. The hope is that students also received an intangible gift that has continued to give. When alumni recognize the role the college played in their substantive, life-changing transformation, their allegiance creates a desire to invest in the transformation of future graduates.

CHAPTER FIVE

In the Company of Others

We asked Michael Bumbry what the primary contributor was to his growth during his four years at college. "The relationships, many of which I hope will be lifelong. Looking back, I think that's probably the best thing that I got out of being here, was the people. All those other things kind of follow." This message was consistent throughout all our interviews with students.

Students are not the only ones to feel that the social environment is important to transformation. Many scholars contend that learning has not been truly transformative unless it results in action within a community. In *Making Their Own Way* (2001), based on a longitudinal study of individuals from college entry into their early thirties, Marcia Baxter Magolda writes about self-authorship. She defines self-authorship as "the ability to collect, interpret, and analyze information and reflect on one's own beliefs in order to form judgments" (14) and suggests that people must answer three questions along this developmental journey:

1. How do I know?
2. Who am I?
3. How do I want to construct relationships with others?

These questions touch on central issues of identity that echo our transformational framework, and the third question is at the heart of this chapter.

Our lives are acted out in social contexts. Our changing selves are played out in relation to others. The word "community" speaks to this shared process in its derivation from the Latin *communis*, meaning service or gift. These social contexts also serve to shape our lives. David Brooks, in an article in the *New York Times* entitled "The Way to Produce a Person"

(June 3, 2013), calls attention to the malleable and adaptive nature of our brains. "Every time you do an activity or have a thought, you are changing yourself into something slightly different than it was before. Every hour you spend with others, you become more like the people around you."

Elon graduate Brian O'Shea talks about the tension he experienced upon his return from his life-changing summer bicycle trip across the country. "When I got back everything was the same as when I left it. I was different but in the same environment again. . . . I learned to take all those relationships that taught me so much over the summer and tried to bring those back here and to help others understand what I learned and the ways that I changed. This either strengthened my relationships with others back on campus or forced a drifting away from some, because I realized that maybe they didn't have the same morals and ethics that I had in life."

The transformative learning process is an interplay between the individual self and others, in effect in all phases of the process—disruption, reflective analysis, verification. In this interplay, the learner is influenced by the community, which, in turn, shapes the individual. The ultimate outcome of this type of learning is action in community, representative of a commitment to a larger purpose. Transformation, then, has the potential to affect a larger group and to contribute not just of the individual but also of the larger community.

Classroom as Community

Because community is a powerful force in the transformative process, the attention that a college gives to the creation of community settings that promote positive growth can have a tremendous payoff. The university's influence on this community begins each year with the admissions process. The existing student body must be familiar enough to attract newcomers but diverse enough to provide a rich potential for dissonance and disequilibrium.

Although the academic curriculum may be what we think of as the heart of the university, Baxter Magolda (2001) points out that shared knowledge making, central to self-authorship, is particularly difficult in the classroom. Academic communities tend to be professor oriented and content driven. The class sizes, schedules, facilities, and other elements of the typical higher education system, she says, are obstacles that make even willing faculty hesitant to shift the pedagogy into shared knowledge making (236). In addition, most students come to college having succeeded in a strongly authoritative—instructor as author instead of student as self-author—educational system, creating an uphill struggle for faculty.

There are, however, steps faculty and administrators can take to make the classroom more conducive to transformative learning. The techniques discussed in previous chapters—such as exposing students to situations and conditions that disrupt their current worldviews, guiding them with deep and provocative questions, providing candid feedback and opportunities for shared dialogue, and encouraging skill and confidence development consistent with their new knowledge—can all be used to enhance the transformative process in the classroom. The evolving beliefs and understandings in one educational area will influence other learning realms as well.

Taking advantage of peer relationships in the classroom is also important. When students observe the problem-solving practices of another student, for instance, the observer benefits as well (Meyer and Land 2006). Baxter Magolda (2001) holds that, contrary to traditional pedagogical assumptions, peers can be valuable contributors to meaning making, even prior to the mastery of a fundamental content of a discipline. Education, she says, must be "more connected by giving students permission to reflect, develop and defend positions, enter the perspectives of their peers, and build on each other's ideas as well as the teacher's" (215).

Creating a variety of types and levels of classroom experiences offers students opportunities to engage at different points in their journey. For many Elon students we interviewed, the required first-year seminar called the "Global Experience" was central to their changing views, but for Nicole Miles, it was the introductory course Elon 101 in her first semester that allowed her to keep going. Though she felt isolated in her dormitory situation, Elon 101 provided her with a small group of people she came to know well and recognize across campus, mitigating her severe homesickness enough that she was able to make it to her next year, when she discovered her great passion for logic and mathematics. "I think it just depends on the person. For me, I really needed that group of people to keep me going."

The creation of specially designed programs can also facilitate growth, providing challenges, support, and opportunities to take action. Shared dialogue is recognized as an important part of the transformative process, and students with common studies, goals, and interests have a ready community for that sharing. Sometimes it is as simple as recognizing that others are experiencing the same emotions and challenges; seeing one's experiences reflected in others removes one from the immediacy of the experience, making awareness of the process itself more likely. Larissa Ferretti, a member of the Honors Program at Elon, comments, "When we are all frustrated in the Honors Program, and that happens a lot, we are all frustrated doing our thesis and we want to strangle ourselves, we're all in that same position. We're all doing it together. So if we complain to one another and are, like, 'Awww, man, I'm in that same position. That really stinks,' we can just relate."

The college must be careful, however, not to focus its whole or best efforts on only certain groups of students. In many cases, students are selected for special programs based on their academic excellence in high school. All students, however, have the potential for transformative learning. In fact, sometimes the "ordinary" student is more likely to make a significant shift than the elite student is.

Clark University, for instance, has developed a number of "communities of effective practice" open to students across campus (Budwig 2013). These communities typically focus on bringing together "multi-generational teams of learners (students, faculty, and others)" to collaboratively explore, and perhaps resolve, important problems within a discipline or in the world. Drawing inspiration from the communities of practice literature (Wenger 1998), these groups work together deliberately to allow disparate groups of people to participate in the community in legitimate but different ways. Undergraduates, of course, do not bring the same expertise to a research group that faculty do, but students can make their own meaningful contributions. Research on the outcomes of Clark's program suggests that "both [students'] intense immersion in a community and their changing roles over time enable students to not only develop the habits of mind but also the repertoires of practice that are essential to leading successful lives. In these communities, students have opportunities to test out the values of a larger community and to fashion their academic, social, and professional identities" (Budwig 2013, 48).

As the Clark University example demonstrates, immersive experiential learning tends to bridge the gap between the classroom and the community. Hands-on experiences most often take place in some kind of relational setting—a different culture during a study abroad experience, for example, a mentoring relationship in research, or the social context inherent in leadership and service learning. These bridges can enable students to make meaning in their learning, to begin to understand, as Baxter Magolda says, not just what they know, but *how* they know.

Amy Rittenour talks about the connection between learning in the classroom, specifically her Global class, and the application in a new social context through study abroad:

> I didn't realize it at the time, but going back to studying abroad, that Global class really helped me prepare my mind-set for being in such a multicultural and diverse society. We were living off of the Middle Eastern hub of London. I'd never seen a woman in a full burka before, and I'm walking to the grocery store and I'm shopping next to these women wearing burkas, and I think if I hadn't had that course, I wouldn't have been as open to it. There are so many different religions there that you are just surrounded by all the time. . . . I think it definitely made me much more receptive to what these people believe and where they come from and again, help me take it all in.

Sometimes the challenge of studying abroad is simply the fact that students must share a space with other people, outside the comfortable spaces they have created back on campus. Larry Basirico, former dean of International Studies at Elon, comments, "Having to live with a group of people in close proximity, having to share spaces and resources, being deprived of 'necessities' such as cell phones, Internet access, air conditioning, or ice in their drinks," he says, "can be very disruptive. Going from living in a comfortable single dorm room to sharing a flat with eight other people interrupts their daily living patterns and creates opportunities for personal growth."

For Michael Bumbry, although he attributes much of his growth to service learning, central to that experience was the effect of a living-learning community: "I would say the Service Learning Community was probably the biggest stretch. For the first time I had a roommate. For the first time I was part of a community and started to understand exactly what community meant. Basically for me that was interacting with people unlike myself, a diverse group."

Professor Tom Arcaro speaks to the connection among students who are Periclean Scholars. Within the larger culture of "me-ness," Arcaro explains, students are dedicating their time and energy to a large project to create global social change. "Why would you do that if you don't get paid or don't get credit? Because it's the right thing to do, and that right action is connected to a larger good. Students are involved in something bigger than themselves. And while there is not necessarily immediate payoff for 'me,' there's a long-term payoff for 'us' . . . and we believe in the power of small acts to further the larger good."

Vertical travel, as mentioned in chapter 4, can even take place without ever moving from place to place at all, if you have community. Tom Arcaro spoke of the Periclean Scholars' AIDS education project in Namibia:

> Some of the students who were most transformed in that class of 2006 didn't go to Namibia at all. But *we* went, because we all worked on the documentaries, we all looked at the photographs, we all watched the interviews. . . . For example, David Dunken never went to Namibia, but David was probably one of the most thoroughly transformed students in that class. He's now in his second year of law school, and whenever I talk to him, he still says that Periclean Scholars gave him a foundation he knows has benefited him greatly. Going there and doing that work is important, but not everybody has to go, especially if a sense of "we" is established.

In experiential learning, sometimes it is the community students connect with in a new place that prompts the greatest shift, and other times it is, as Brian O'Shea alluded to, the community they leave behind after their return home. When asked if there was ever a moment in college in which she thought, "I've changed," Olivia Hubert-Allen answered in the affirmative, saying it was at the end of her experience in her internship abroad. "I don't know if it was a fear or something I was proud of at the time. It was sort of at the end of my study abroad experience. I kind of felt like I didn't really know who I was anymore. I had gone abroad. I had abandoned some of the characteristics that had been a part of my personality for a very long time and sort of taken on new aspects. At first I thought, 'I don't know if I like this new person I have become. Is this how I want to be?' I've sort of grown into that now. When I came back there was some culture shock. I think I got back some of my old characteristics, but I also kept a lot of what I got while I was abroad. Now I'm somewhere in between who I was there and who I am here." Significantly, her attention to relationships played an important role in her experience. "I kind of was on my own. It was the first time that I really felt disconnected from my friends and family." It was only with this break from the relationships she had previously relied on that Olivia felt able to explore a significant shift in who she wanted to be.

Larissa Ferretti cites relationships with faculty during her research experience as a key factor in her college experience. "I lived in the Honors Pavilion the first two years of college, and we take one class a semester together. . . . I've been involved in campus organizations, but for me they were more of a social, fun thing to do. I don't think they really stretched me to think beyond myself. Not that they can't, but that for me they didn't. But my relationship with faculty members here definitely has. . . . Dr. Vandermaas-Peeler and I . . . have a really good relationship. She pushes me to think harder on things."

Community beyond the Classroom

Many of the lasting impressions of college life take place outside the academic curriculum. Cocurricular programs are fundamentally about students in community, such things as where they live and activities they do with each other. The mission of Elon's Division of Student Life is similar to that at other institutions: to prepare students to be independent, lifelong learners and productive, responsible community members.

In a residential college, where and how students live is an enormous factor that can work for or against transformation. Living-learning communities are an example of an intentional use of student residence, intersecting physical and educational structures, to foster meaningful student interaction. These learning communities bring students together with staff and faculty in the same residential area, united by a common interest, cause, or purpose. With residents taking some of the same courses, bridging of in-class learning and out-of-class experiences pervades the environment. This yields a synergistic effect that enhances both types of experiences, promoting learning whenever and wherever it might occur. Research has demonstrated that living-learning communities with these characteristics deepen both critical thinking skills and civic engagement and help students make a smoother academic and social transition from high school to college (Brower and Inkelas 2010) and, we hope, from college to life beyond.

Student Lisa Bodine ties her residence in a living-learning community to the important intertwining of classroom and residential conversation: "It put me in an environment where discussions we had in class would continue on into the dorm. We'd have these really great conversations about things we'd done in Global or in our team-taught courses and just continue the discussions." Lisa goes on: "Those discussions were huge in our friendships. When I look back on freshman year, our first semester, it was the most eclectic group of people. Whenever we get together now, I just think, what a weird group of individuals. But we gelled. We just clicked together because we learned so much in our Global class and kept talking about it later."

Amy Rittenour, too, lived in a learning community: "It was great because although high school was okay for me, I was kind of bored. I grew up in a very rural area, so there was a pasture across the street from my high school; it wasn't very exciting. But I got here and there were people from all across the country. I was living in the Honors pavilion. We had people from ten or twelve different states, all different levels, from all different majors, and yet we could all come together. We were all kind of in the same boat. It made it really exciting for me to be here."

Olivia lived in a learning community for communications students: "For me, it was a tremendous experience. I was around all of these communications geeks who checked the Internet and blogs constantly and could talk about Supreme Court and news. It was exciting to be for the first time around people who I thought were like me. . . . I sort of had a hard time making friends in classes, but I did a really good job of making friends on my hall the first couple of weeks."

On the one hand, student organizations also can play a strong role in students' feelings of safety and belonging, their exposure to differences, and their opportunities to build their confidence and skills. On the other hand, they can sometimes foster negative attitudes and behaviors through a kind of pack mentality, what some scholars refer to as "hyperbonding," when a group becomes "empowered around their own norms of immature behavior, sloppy work, and incivility" (Smith et al. 2004, 102). Again, it is the interplay between individual growth and social interactions that fosters the most positive change.

Some scholars associate the Greek system with a "party pathway" through the undergraduate years "built around an implicit agreement between the university and students to demand little of each other" (Armstrong and Hamilton 2013, 15). For Sarah Gould, it was leaving behind those relationships that allowed her to move forward and to align her new values and commitments with her daily actions and interactions. But Greek societies were central to the transformative experience for some students, such as Michael Bumbry, because of the relationships they provided and the role those relationships played in the balance of safety and challenge during the disruption and critical reflection times of transformative learning.

Regardless of a campus's particular culture, activities—formal and informal—and college traditions—official and unofficial—fill the interstitial spaces of college life. College faculty, staff, and administrators have a role both in designing some of these activities and in responding to ones generated from outside their bounds. How administrators respond to students' actions and behaviors as they find their way along their journey sends powerful messages regarding both the values and expectations of the college and the limits of tolerance. What is the response to a student protest during the busiest week of prospective student visits? How does the college respond to the expression of biases against different groups?

Many of these responses must be spontaneous and reactive. There are some troubling behaviors, however, that are ongoing and can be addressed through the lens of student transformation. Elon, like many other colleges across the United States, struggles with excess alcohol consumption among its students. When a presidential task force was assigned to explore the problem and offer ways to address it, its members came at the problem from multiple perspectives. Education about alcohol use was a central component but, recognizing the importance of shared meaning making, that education was designed to come from peers; this approach builds on research about the power of social norms (e.g., Irwin and Simpson 2013). The task force also recognized that alcohol was serving important purposes for students, such as providing a social lubricant. If alcohol use were to decrease, something would need to take its place. What can the college offer to fill the voids? Alcohol use tends to be linked to issues of community. Relationship-building activities, late-night eating and lounging spaces that foster conversation, and physically demanding activities, for example, can offer social venues that do not rely on alcohol use.

In 2009, Georgetown University attempted to reduce alcohol-related harm to undergraduates through a highly visible social norms campaign. The "You Don't Know Jack" promotional materials paired entertaining facts about the university's mascot, Jack, with relatively unknown statistics about students and alcohol at Georgetown. A small group calling itself SMURF, Students Marketing Under-Recognized Facts, helped to design and implement the campaign. Data from the National College Health Assessment Survey suggest that this campaign produced some positive outcomes related to moderating and monitoring student alcohol consumption (National Social Norms Institute, n.d.).

For many students, excessive alcohol consumption and other risky behaviors are something of a rite of passage in college, a ritual for transitioning from one status to another: from outside a social group to inside it or from one side of a line of demarcation to another, in this case, from childhood to adulthood. Inherent in most traditional rites of passage is some danger that speaks of life and death, often with a person being symbolically reborn into a new role or status. This danger or crisis calls into question one's identity and even existence. Survival of this crisis brings the privilege of belonging, affiliation with an exclusive group; the isolation of the initiation rite promotes an increased desire for that affiliation and group bonding. Without healthier opportunities to make this journey, people in this developmental stage sometimes create their own daring events, hazing peers in a social group or driving while intoxicated. If the social environment of the emerging adult does not provide significant, identity-challenging situations, students will look for ways to create them on their own with whatever tools, such as alcohol, they have available to them.

Community Spaces

Institutions communicate values within the community not just through their activities but through their physical and temporal spaces as well. The physical spaces of the college convey values that shape the community. Consider the architecture visible on a campus. Wake Forest University has a unified architecture intentionally rooted in the neo-Georgian style, marked by symmetry and a sense of order and tradition, of dynamic stability. Oberlin College's architecture, in contrast, is an eclectic collection of buildings representing the architectural trends and the social concerns of the time, consistent with its reputation for being socially progressive.

Physical spaces often become symbols associated with students' growth and change as well. Professor Niedzela says it is at the end of the sophomore year when some biology majors make the significant shift to seeing themselves as scientists, a change they identify with McMichael building, the building where so much of their work toward this change has taken place. "They've survived all our required biology courses, they've survived general chemistry and organic chemistry, and they start identifying themselves as scientists and start choosing the direction they want to go. They have a lot of peer support; it's kind of a badge of honor to be in McMichael for many, many hours." Creating buildings specifically dedicated to housing certain values also sends social messages. Elon's recent construction of an interfaith center within an academic pavilion, for example, was an intentional valuing of a quest for both spiritual and intellectual enlighten-ment, supporting understanding, reconciliation, justice, and charity. Even the absence of physical constructions—the presence of intentional green space—is a message shared within the community.

The dedication of what is perhaps the most valuable college resource, time, is another way the institution promotes social values. These tempo-ral spaces also draw student activity and can be used to intentionally build support for exploration of dissonance, shared dialogue, deep inquiry about assumptions, and venues for reaching out, trying out new behaviors, living out new life choices. At Elon, for example, having dedicated weekly time for College Coffee—a gathering of students, faculty, and staff over light refreshments—both fosters opportunities for connections and symbolizes the university's commitment to community. While such rituals might seem extraneous, they can be powerful when a crisis arises that can test a community. On the morning of September 11, 2001, for instance, people from throughout the Elon community knew where to gather if they wanted to reflect together on the unfolding tragedy—they came to Col-lege Coffee.

Manuel Gomez (2008) at the University of California–Irvine (UCI) has taken a similar approach to building community by focusing, perhaps ironically, on highly contentious issues on campus, including "the inter-sections of religion, politics, and national identity." UCI's highly diverse student body had a reputation for being politically sedate until the early 2000s until a series of events, starting with a University of California Re-gents' decision on affirmative action followed by unrelated conflicts be-tween Jewish and Muslim students on campus. While the campus roiled, Vice-chancellor Gomez helped to implement a Difficult Dialogues initia-tive including both curricular and co-curricular programs that gave stu-dents opportunities to experience challenging but civic discourse. Over time, the results of this program confirmed Gomez's belief that "the more our students learn how to learn about conflict, contention, and contro-versy, the less difficult these dialogues may eventually become. Certainly students need a safe place in which to learn, a civil community. But a com-munity is not safe when speech is chilled and certain ideas are not free to be heard, examined, and evaluated" (2008, 17).

Creating a Norm of Transformation

By attending to community in all these different areas of college life, the institution develops an atmosphere in which the transformative process is to some extent self-driven; a social norm of transformative learning is created. When students are surrounded by a community that is moving in the direction of transformation, there is an inertia that tends to pull people forward. This ability to establish an expectation of personal commitment to growth among members of a group is an extremely powerful force.

Larissa Ferretti knew when she came to Elon that she was going to study abroad. "When you come to Elon the question is not really, 'Are you going to study abroad?' It's, 'When are you going to go?' because everyone does it. When you first come here, that sounds like a lot, to be in another country, but I was surrounded by friends. . . . They were all doing it. When I was in that environment, I thought, 'This is a little uncomfortable, but Sally did it last year. I have seen other people do it; I know I can do it too.'"

When their peers are stretching themselves, are openly navigating the waters of disequilibrium, are challenging their own assumptions and the assumptions of others, and are reaching to build new skills and abilities, there is an implied expectation that others will follow suit. At the same time, an important social support is created for those endeavors. This shared awareness can also help students manage the emotional and intellectual ambiguity that accompanies deep change. When Larissa returned from her studies in Guatemala and then in Italy, she turned to her Elon peers who had also gone abroad. "I had friends all over the world, Paris, Africa, Peru. . . . They were all experiencing the same things. . . . You're going through this re-initiation into the United States. You don't really know if you're feeling the right feelings, what you are supposed to be feeling. It's kind of an awkward time period. My family couldn't really relate to that because none of them have studied abroad. That was a time that I would go to my friends."

The more this process is woven into the fabric of the institution—the more students are taking enlightened action within the college community—the richer the college environment itself becomes. Students are thinking creatively and taking leadership roles. They are inspiring their peers with their own experiences, insights, and courage. Their actions call to the best in those around them.

Without a norm of transformation, students (and faculty and staff) may tire of disorientation and change. Unaided, they may fall back to previous habits, even when the new possibility is promising. In some cases, moving past resistance requires an outside influence. A conducive environment can help pull a person along the desired path, past the point of resistance. For Jill, it was the support of her personal network at home and her budding community on campus that kept her from leaving college after a sexual assault by a classmate during first-year orientation. "It was my friends, it was the organizations I joined," she says, that made her able to stay.

Intentionally creating a community that has momentum in the desired direction becomes a self-perpetuating force. Finding ways for students to tell their stories of transformation confirms its value to the individual and communicates its value to peers. An essential part of this awareness building is dialogue about the *process*. For example, when students reflect on and share their experiences abroad, in service, in leadership, or in research, we should encourage students to talk not just about how they changed as a result but what the ongoing experience was like for them. What was the hardest part? How did it feel? How did they resolve their struggles?

Redefining Home

When Thomas Wolfe declared, "You can't go home again," he spoke to the one-way journey of growing up. It is true, one can never return to the home of one's past, but "home" can get redefined. Going home—or being home—can become a new and different experience. Sharon Parks (2011) reminds us, "To be at home is to be able to make meaning . . . that holds over time even through intermediate events."

In this sense, "home" becomes internalized. When transformation is realized during the college years, students emerge with an internalized and expanded sense of home, one they can take with them wherever they go and from which they can be ongoing agents of transformation in the world. Internalizing this sense of "home" empowers them to be at home in a much larger world and to respond to its needs in a fuller way. The person engaged in transformative learning must not only be moved but must also be moved *to* something. The responsibility to a larger commitment that characterizes transformative learning calls for considered action within a social context. Exercising this responsibility enhances our "response-ability."

A long-term hope of an alma mater is that graduates will look back on their experiences and recognize an essence of home and that they will be carrying that sense of home with them no matter how far away they venture from the physical locus of their college. In an educational process that is not merely informative but transformative, that hope is fulfilled. "Home" is no longer the place they left to come to college. Home is an internalized ability to face the vicissitudes of life with thoughtfulness, insight, and compassion.

Sustaining the Practice

How do we encourage and support graduates in their newfound way of being in the world, both in sustaining the changes they experienced in college and in continuing on a path of ongoing transformation? According to Baxter Magolda (2001), not much self-authorship occurs during the college years, but we can jumpstart the process, increasing the success of that process in the young adult years, a time when, Baxter Magolda points out, the learning is less compressed in time but when the consequences of *not* learning have more far-reaching ramifications.

Within their undergraduate years, we can do our best to equip students with both an experience of transformation and an awareness of, and appreciation for, the transformative process itself. Faculty and staff can have conversations with students, not just about what they need to *do* to succeed in college, but they can ask questions: What does it mean to succeed? What does it mean to become a scientist? To become a leader? To be a global citizen? What role do your relationships play in that becoming?

As students transition from their college environments as young adults understanding the importance of community, we hope they will be intentional in choosing relationships and social contexts that will support their changes and bring them along on this journey. It's easy for students to see their years of college as a discrete unit of time, one in which they have a chance to experiment with behaviors and identities before they return to their norm. When they see their graduation as entry into the "real world," the implication is that their four years of learning were suspended in artificiality. Perhaps the most powerful way to reach beyond these four years is to make the college years as real as possible for the students. Address the big questions. Dig down into the meaning and teach them to act.

Sarah Gould, who, over the course of her time at Elon, developed a passion for teaching disadvantaged children in Title I schools, learned through mentoring and service activities what could be done to change that. Eventually, she came to believe that she was capable of making those changes happen, even when her parents questioned her decision.

> The biggest part of it is that sense of power. . . . I could imagine myself actually having an impact. . . . I called my mom after class one day and said, "I think I want to teach in a Title I school." At first she said, "You're crazy. You are crazy! Do you know all the barriers you're going to face, and how hard it's going to be, and how exhausting? I don't want you to get burned out and not love to teach." I remember telling her, "Okay, yes, that could happen, but I think I could handle it. I think I could deal with whatever situations come up." I don't remember exactly what she said, but it was something to the effect of, "If you want to do it then that's great; I'm going to support you."

The students in our interviews spoke of the absolutely essential role relationships played throughout all stages of their transformative learning process. The presence and input of others challenged them to new levels of thinking and understanding and allowed them to feel safe and comfortable enough to continue with their journeys. It was the presence of others, quietly one-on-one, in small or large groups, or in public forums, that allowed them to act on their new awareness and build their skills and confidence. And it was the tug of relationships that helped them see the importance of a thoughtfully chosen social context to sustaining their newfound values and abilities.

The university cannot—should not—control what company the students keep. But if we want our students to be likely to have transformative experiences, we should support community infrastructures conducive to positive change.

The college experience is often referred to as a journey. Parks (2011), however, prefers the word "pilgrimage," a concept that is deeply interdependent with that of home. A journey involves travel, but a pilgrimage conjures images of a long trip in search of higher meaning and an eventual return home, enriched with greater wisdom and blessings. Some of our greatest literature tells the stories of people who leave home in search of something great but, in the end, find it within themselves. Such are the stories we hope for our students.

CHAPTER SIX

From Individuals to Institutions

Any university wishing to thrive must continue to evolve. But make no mistake—there is a difference between relentlessly creating new initiatives and fostering ongoing transformation. Charlton Ogburn (1957) captured the practice of many institutions when he wrote about his experiences in the Burma Campaign in World War II: "Perhaps because we are so good at organizing, we tend . . . to meet any new situation by reorganizing; and a wonderful method it can be for creating the illusion of progress while producing confusion, inefficiency, and demoralization."

Sustaining transformation does not mean doing the same thing over and over, but neither does it refer to change for the sake of change. Because newness creates excitement and often media coverage, it is easy for institutions to become almost addicted to change—a very different experience from being committed to transformation.

Transformation is often preceded by significant events but is usually only evident in retrospect. In its midst, it may look like chaos and uncertainty, as changes are taking place in small increments, one decision at a time. We must be patient because there will be moments—many of them—in which what is happening looks messy or even misguided rather than inspired or promising. Those involved need to know that as long as they are guided by a core sense of self and mission and are open to what emerges, the successful journey through disruptive events and seemingly chaotic times eventually shows itself to be a critical opportunity for transformation.

Like any university experiencing growth, Elon is grappling to manage the tension between its changes and its core identity. It is our hope that this struggle will *not* be resolved soon. Transformative learning is an open-ended process; one never "arrives." This ongoing question—how does an organization or an individual grow, yet maintain an authentic sense of identity?—is the most essential part of the process.

Both problems and their solutions need to be identified from the ground up; that is, they need to emerge from observations and reports of what is and isn't working in the context of your institution, rather than being imposed from above or imported from external sources. Yet at the same time, it can be very helpful to learn what is working for, or has failed at, other similar institutions. Of course, solutions on one campus rarely can be transferred completely into a new context, but models and ideas can present visions of the possible, allowing creative faculty, staff, and students to devise new or refine existing campus programs to meet emerging needs.

The university is what it is because of past actions and practices, and, at the same time, our current actions and practices are creating our future identities. The identity we create is at once stable and dynamic. In order to "stay the same," we must constantly be responding to internal and external challenges while supporting functions essential to the institution's integrity.

Over time and with practice, the continued integration of dissonance, honest examination, and recalibrating actions will strengthen the university's core, representing institutional depth and soul. When a university's energy is poured into its central purpose rather than spun out on popular trends, the benefits and returns are compounded. In investing in its true mission, the institution challenges individual members of its community to recognize and act upon their own purposes and values, transforming the university into a body that is greater than the sum of its parts.

When presented with this "practice what you preach" proposition, some people counter that not everyone needs to be transformed, especially when they are long past their own formative college years. But for both organisms and organizations, there is no such thing as staying completely still; we are always in the process of becoming. The more intentional we are about the processes, the more rewarding the outcomes are likely to be.

Stories of Transformation

The stories of our institutions are a valuable source of insight. Just as the students' stories in this book capture transformative learning in a way that theoretical writing alone cannot, the stories we tell ourselves and others about our university reveal truths that might otherwise be inaccessible.

We tell our stories in many different ways. Most obvious are the messages we send through formal or public communications such as websites, university ceremonies, and published histories of the institution. In 2000, when the new Belk Library at Elon opened, the arcade lining the front of the building displayed a series of photo engravings marking significant events in the university's history. Images such as these not only capture but create and sustain the lore—for example, the fire that destroyed Elon's Main Building, including classrooms, library, and chapel, and, seventy-seven years later, the adoption of a new mascot, the Phoenix rising from the ashes.

More effective at revealing the subtler messages and deeper currents of change, perhaps, are the stories shared in hallways, over coffee, or as digressions in meetings. George Keller noted in *Transforming a College,* published in 2004 and reissued in 2014, that Elon has changed considerably in recent decades, as evidenced by the occasional reference to "old Elon" overheard in conversations among faculty and staff. At a summer writing retreat organized by the University's Center for the Advancement of Teaching and Learning, faculty from different disciplines gathered off campus to work on writing projects, taking breaks as needed to wander the grounds and share thoughts about their work with colleagues. "This feels like 'old Elon,'" more than one faculty member observed, relishing the unpressured time for reflection and communication with colleagues.

The contrast, of course, is to "new Elon," the perceived reality of the present, where the number of employees has increased by more than 50 percent since 2001, and demands on faculty to engage in substantive scholarship and on staff to manage the resources necessary to support a vibrant student body have also increased. In "old Elon," all of the faculty and staff seemed to know everyone else. Now it's hard to walk across campus without seeing many unfamiliar faces. Faculty still know their students by name, but not as many invite their students over for dinner each semester, a common practice in "old Elon." The past, however, is never perfect; "old Elon" had larger class sizes and heavier teaching loads, less diversity among the students and faculty, lower salaries, and fewer resources, and no Center for the Advancement of Teaching and Learning to sponsor such retreats. The point is not which story is "true" or even which "Elon" is better. It is the story within the story that we listen for. Perhaps this story tells us that we value our sense of community, our contemplative time with colleagues, and our personal connections and, as the campus is growing, that we are open to new avenues to foster those qualities.

Like all colleges and universities, Elon tells stories of student success. The stories we tell about our students, however, are also stories about us as institutions and about our aspirations. Do we trumpet the student who wins a highly competitive scholarship because we seek national recognition? Or do we single out the student who was granted an opportunity to study with a renowned scholar because we value disciplinary scholarship? Or the one who contributed an extraordinary number of volunteer hours because the service ethic is foremost among the university's values? Perhaps it is the once-lackluster first-year student who found her passion in journalism and, to the surprise of her parents, landed a relevant job after college, because the magnitude of her transformation and the depth of her self-discovery, rather than the magnitude of the honor itself, resonates deeply with the university's mission.

Institutional leaders must walk a fine line between promoting a public image and questioning that image, between being an advocate for something and being critical of it. Because stories are so powerful, we must find ways to search out those we would never hear in our usual circles. In particular, accounts of events and anecdotal lore shared by people with less positional power can provide insights into the internal vulnerabilities of the institution. (There is great power, though certainly not great joy, in hearing that the emperor has no clothes!) These stories are told freely in the safety of groups of like-minded people but tend to be withheld, or at least greatly tamed, when shared in the presence of university leaders.

Examining an institution's stories is not about controlling the stories but about listening with an open heart and mind. We must open ourselves to stories we would normally not want to hear. Often these stories accuse us; they tend to be stories of discrimination, unfairness, of overworking and undervaluing, and of not being understood. We tend, of course, to dismiss stories that are clearly biased or skewed. Yet even stories that are inaccurate or distorted are told for a reason, and those reasons may offer us insights. The story may have a message beyond the self-serving needs or victim persona of the messenger.

Furthermore, it may be that some stories do not ring true because we have assumed a truth that does not allow for that possibility. Permitting the intrusion of this "false" reality into what we already "know" to be true is the beginning of transformation. What if it were true? What would we know about ourselves, what would we do to address this, to bring it into alignment with our vision of our institution?

Institutional Transformation

Much of this book is about exploring tensions without necessarily resolving them. Institutions would also do well to give themselves some breathing room in undertaking their own transformative processes. The process is messy and unpredictable, creating the type of atmosphere most managers are trained to resolve as swiftly as possible. It may initially seem awkward—and scary—as is the development of expertise in any area. The wobbliness with which one first attempts to maintain a forward path on a bicycle, however, slowly gives way to grace and power. Soon focus can be given to climbing hills, dodging potholes, jumping curbs, and just enjoying the ride.

In many ways, it is even more challenging for an institution than for an individual person to persist in the transformative process, given the number of people who have to share in an organization's commitment to make it happen. It is particularly challenging when the primary focus of that process is an ever-changing student population. But as the challenge is multiplied, so are the rewards.

A university cannot compel or guarantee transformative learning for its students or for its faculty and staff. But leaders in higher education *can* provide a fertile environment for meaningful transformation. Our goal is for our students to become their own universities, integrating what they have learned into their daily lives and internalizing the transformative process and thus continuing to grow long after they leave the classrooms, residence halls, and lawns of the college campus. In essence, alumni become the embodiment of the university.

Transformative learning, when undertaken by the university itself, brings the transformative process to life for college students. When students and university personnel alike are steeped in an atmosphere of thoughtful transformation, the experience becomes more powerful for all involved. By making this type of learning integral to its very way of being, the institution brings a higher level of integrity to the process: the integrity of doing what one professes. It is this integrity that brings the strength and vitality to the educational process that allows us to truly fulfil our mission.

Allen, Tammy D., and Lillian T. Eby, eds. 2010. *The Blackwell Handbook of Mentoring: A Multiple Perspectives Approach*. Hoboken, NJ: Wiley-Blackwell.

Armstrong, Elizabeth A., and Laura T. Hamilton. 2009. *Paying for the Party: How College Maintains Inequality*. Cambridge, MA: Harvard University Press.

Arnett, Jeffrey. 2004. *Emerging Adulthood: The Winding Road from Late Teens through the Twenties*. New York: Oxford University Press.

Arum, Richard, and Josipa Roksa. 2010. *Academically Adrift: Limited Learning on College Campuses*. Chicago: University of Chicago Press.

Bain, Ken. 2004. *What the Best College Teachers Do*. Cambridge, MA: Harvard University Press.

Baumgartner, Lisa M. 2002. Living and learning with HIV/AIDS: Transformational tales continued. *Adult Education Quarterly* 53: 44–70.

Baxter Magolda, Marcia B. 2001. *Making Their Own Way: Narratives for Transforming Higher Education to Promote Self-Development*. Sterling, VA: Stylus.

Baxter Magolda, Marcia B., and Patricia M. King, eds. 2004. *Learning Partnerships: Theory and Models of Practice to Education for Self-Authorship*. Sterling, VA: Stylus.

Berry, Wendell. 1987. *Home Economics*. New York: North Point Press.

Bowleg, Lisa. 2008. When Black + lesbian + woman ≠ Black lesbian woman: The methodological challenges of qualitative and quantitative intersectionality research. *Sex Roles* 59: 312–25.

Boyd, Robert D. 1991. *Personal Transformations in Small Groups*. New York: Routledge.

Boyd, Robert D., and J. Gordon Myers. 1988. Transformative education. *International Journal of Lifelong Education* 7(4): 261–84.

Braskamp, Larry A., Lois C. Trautvetter, and Kelly Ward. 2006. *Putting Students First: How Colleges Develop Students Purposefully*. Bolton, MA: Anker.

Brock, Sabra. 2011. Tools for change: A quantitative examination of transformative learning and its precursor steps among undergraduate students. Presented at the Ninth International Conference on Transformative Learning, Athens, Greece, May 28–29.

Brookfield, Stephen. 2012. *Teaching for Critical Thinking: Tools and Techniques to Help Students Question Their Assumptions.* San Francisco: Jossey-Bass.

Brookfield, Stephen P., and Stephen Preskill. 2005. *Discussion as a Way of Teaching: Tools and Techniques for Democratic Classrooms,* 2nd ed. San Francisco: Jossey-Bass.

Brooks, David. 2013. The way to produce a person *New York Times,* June 3.

Brower, Aaron. M., and Karen K. Inkelas. 2010. Living-learning programs: One high-impact educational practice we know a lot about. *Liberal Education* 96:2(Spring): 36–43.

Budwig, Nancy. 2013. The learning sciences and liberal education. *Change* (May–June): 40–48.

Bureau, Dan., Helen G. Ryan, Chad Ahren, Rick Shoup, and Vasti Torres. 2011. Student learning in fraternities and sororities: Using NSSE data to describe members' participation in educationally meaningful activities in college. *Oracle* 6(1): 1–22.

Carnes, Mark C. 2005. Inciting speech. *Change* 37(2): 6–11.

Carnes, Mark. 2011. Setting students' minds on fire. *Chronicle of Higher Education,* March 6.

Carter, Terry J. 2002. The importance of talk to midcareer women's development: A collaborative inquiry. *The Journal of Business Communication* 39: 55–91.

Chickering, Arthur W., Jon C. Dalton, and Liesa Stamm. 2006. *Encouraging Authenticity and Spirituality in Higher Education.* San Francisco: Jossey-Bass.

Chickering, Arthur W., and Linda Reisser. 1993. *Education and Identity,* 2nd ed. San Francisco: Jossey-Bass.

Chism, Nancy Van Note. 2006. Challenging traditional assumptions and rethinking learning spaces. In *Learning Spaces,* edited by Diana G. Oblinger. EDUCAUSE, Indiana University-Purdue University Indianapolis and Indiana University. http://net.educause.edu/ir/library/pdf/pub7102b.pdf.

Clydesdale, Tim. 2007. *The First Year Out: Understanding American Teens after High School (Morality and Society Series).* Chicago: University of Chicago Press.

Colby, Anne, Thomas Ehrlich, Elizabeth Beaumont, and Jason Stephens. 2003. *Educating Citizens: Preparing America's Undergraduates for Lives of Moral and Civic Responsibility.* San Francisco: Jossey-Bass.

Cole, Darnell. 2008. Constructive criticism: The role of student-faculty interactions on African American and Hispanic students' educational gains. *Journal of College Student Development* 49(6): 587–605.

Collier, Amy, William Watson, and Arturo Ozuna. 2011. ClassroomNEXT: Engaging faculty and students in learning space design. *EDUCAUSE Learning Initiative Brief* (July). http://net.educause.edu/ir/library/pdf/ELIB1102.pdf.

DeSimone, Jeffrey S. 2010. Fraternity membership and frequent drinking. *National Bureau of Economic Research Working Paper* 16291 (August). http://papers.ssrn.com/sol3/papers.cfm?abstract_id=1662285.

Dewey, John. 1997. *Experience and Education.* New York: Free Press.

Dirkx, John M. 2003. Images, transformative learning, and the work of soul. *Adult Learning,* 12(3): 15–16.

Doorley, Scott, and Scott Witthoft. 2012. *Make Space: How to Set the Stage for Creative Collaboration.* San Francisco: Jossey-Bass.

Duke University Student Affairs, Sophomore Year Experience (SYE). n.d. http://studentaffairs.duke.edu/hdrl/sophomores-juniors-seniors/sophomore-year-experience-sye.

Easwaran, Ecknath. 2010. *Words to Live By: Short Readings of Daily Wisdom,* 4th ed. Tomales, CA: Nilgiri Press.

Evans, Nancy J., Deanna S. Forney, Florence M. Guido, Lori D. Patton, and Kristen A. Renn. 2010. *Student Development in College: Theory, Research, and Practice.* 2nd ed. San Francisco: Jossey-Bass.

Felten, Peter, H., Dirksen L. Bauman, Aaron Kheriaty, and Edward Taylor. 2013. *Transformative Conversations: A Guide to Mentoring Communities among Colleagues in Higher Education.* San Francisco: Jossey-Bass.

Flores, Ronald J. O., Catherine Crosby-Currie, and Christine Zimmerman. 2007. Engaged pedagogies, civic development, and student well-being within a liberal learning context. *Peer Review* 9(Summer): 3.

Freire, Paulo. 1970. *Pedagogy of the Oppressed.* New York: Seabury Press.

Gawande, Atul. 2009. *The Checklist Manifesto: How to Get Things Right.* New York: Henry Holt.

Greenfield, Gerald M., Jennifer R. Keup, and John N. Gardner. 2013. *Developing and Sustaining Successful First-Year Programs: A Guide for Practitioners.* San Francisco: Jossey-Bass.

Gomez, Manuel N. 2008. Imagining the future: Cultivating civility in a field of discontent. *Change* March–April: 10–17.

Hart Research Associates. 2013. It takes more than a major: Employer priorities for college learning and student success. *Liberal Education* 99(2). http://www.aacu.org/liberaleducation/le-sp13/hartresearchassociates.cfm

Henscheid, Jean M. 2012. Senior seminars and capstone courses. In *The Senior Year: Culminating Experiences and Transitions,* edited by Mary S. Hunter, Jennifer R. Keup, Jillian Kinzie, and Heather Maietta, 91–109. Columbia, SC: National Resource Center.

Hunt, Celia, 2013. *Transformative Learning through Creative Life Writing.* New York: Routledge.

Hunter, Mary S., Barbara F. Tobolowsky, and John N. Gardner. 2009. *Helping Sophomores Succeed: Understanding and Improving the Second-Year Experience.* San Francisco: Jossey-Bass.

Huston, Therese A., and Michele DiPietro. 2007. In the eye of the storm: Students' perceptions of faculty actions following a collective tragedy. In *To Improve the Academy,* vol. 25, *Resources for Faculty, Instructional and Organizational Develop-*

ment, edited by D. R. Robertson and L. B. Nilson, 207–24. Bolton, MA: Anker Publishing.

Irwin, Kyle, and Brent Simpson. 2013. Do descriptive norms solve social dilemmas? Conformity and contributions in collective action groups. *Social Forces,* doi:10.1093/sf/sos196.

Johnson, W. Brad. 2006. *On Being a Mentor: A Guide for Higher Education Faculty.* New York: Psychology Press.

Josselson, Ruthellen. 1996. *Revising Herself: The Story of Women's Identity from College to Midlife.* New York: Oxford University Press.

Kegan, Robert. 1982. *The Evolving Self: Problem and Process in Human Development.* Cambridge, MA: Harvard University Press.

Kegan, Robert, and Lisa Lahey. 2009. *Immunity to Change.* Cambridge, MA: Harvard Business School Publishing.

Keller, George. 2014. *Transforming a College: The Story of a Little-Known College's Strategic Climb to National Distinction,* 2nd ed. Baltimore: Johns Hopkins University Press.

King, Kathleen. 2004. Both sides now: Examining transformative learning and professional development of educators. *Innovative Higher Education* 29: 155–74.

King, Patricia M., and Karen S. Kitchener. 1994. *Developing Reflective Judgment: Understanding and Promoting Intellectual Growth and Critical Thinking in Adolescents and Adults.* San Francisco: Jossey-Bass.

Kuh, George. 2003. What we're learning about student engagement from NSSE. *Change* 35(2): 24–32.

Kuh, George D. 2008. *High-Impact Educational Practices: What Are They, Who Has Access to Them, and Why They Matter.* Washington, DC: Association of American Colleges and Universities.

Lewin, Ross, ed. 2009. *The Handbook of Practice and Research in Study Abroad: Higher Education and the Quest for Global Citizenship.* New York: Routledge.

Light, Richard. 2004. *Making the Most of College: Students Speak Their Minds.* Cambridge, MA: Harvard University Press.

Light, Tracy P., Helen L. Chen, Helen L, and John C. Ittelson. 2012. *Documenting Learning with ePortfolios: A Guide for College Instructors.* San Francisco: Jossey-Bass.

Loeb, Paul R. 1999. *Soul of a Citizen: Living with Conviction in a Cynical Time.* New York: St. Martin's Press.

Manor, Chris, Stephen Bloch-Schulman, Kelly Flannery, and Peter Felten. 2010. Foundations of student-faculty partnerships in the scholarship of teaching and learning. In *Engaging Student Voices in the Study of Teaching and Learning,* edited by C. Werder and M. M. Otis, 3–15. Sterling, VA: Stylus.

Markus, Hazel, and Paula Nirius. 1986. Possible selves. *American Psychologist* 4(41): 954–69.

Merriam, Sharan B. 2004. The role of cognitive development in Mezirow's transformational learning theory. *Adult Education Quarterly* 55(1): 60–68.

Meyer, Jan H. F., and Ray Land. 2006. *Overcoming Barriers to Student Understanding: Threshold Concepts and Troublesome Knowledge.* New York: Routledge.

Mezirow, Jack. 1991. *Transformative Dimensions of Adult Learning.* San Francisco: Jossey-Bass.

Mezirow, Jack. 1995. Transformative theory in adult learning. In *In Defense of the Lifeworld,* edited by M. Walton, 39–70. Albany, NY: SUNY Press.

Mezirow, Jack. 2000. *Learning as Transformation: Critical Perspectives on a Theory in Progress.* Jossey-Bass Higher and Adult Education Series. San Francisco: Jossey Bass.

Mezirow, Jack, and Edward Taylor, eds. 2009. *Transformative Learning in Practice: Insights from Community, Workplace, and Higher Education.* San Francisco: Jossey-Bass.

Monahan, Torin. 2002. Flexible space and built pedagogy: Emerging IT embodiments, *Inventio.* http://www.doit.gmu.edu/inventio/past/display_past.asp?pID= spring02&sID=monahan.

Moore, Thomas. 2008. *A Life at Work: The Joy of Discovering What You Were Born to Do.* New York: Broadway Books.

Morris, Libby V., and Randy L. Swing. 2005. Elon University: Transforming education through a community of inquiry and engagement. In *Achieving and Sustaining Institutional Excellence for the First Year of College,* edited by Betsy O. Barefoot, John N. Gardner, Marc Cutright, Libby V. Morris, Charles C Schroeder, Stephen W. Schwartz, Michael J. Siegel, and Randy L. Swing, 166–90. San Francisco: Jossey-Bass.

National Social Norms Institute. n.d. Case study: Georgetown University. http://www.socialnorms.org/CaseStudies/georgetown.php.

Ogburn, Charlton. 1957. Merrill's marauders. *Harper's.*

Palmer, Parker J., and Arthur Zajonc. 2010. *The Heart of Higher Education: A Call to Renewal.* San Francisco: Jossey-Bass.

Parks, Sharon. 2011. *Big Questions, Worthy Dreams: Mentoring Emerging Adults in Their Search for Meaning, Purpose, and Faith,* 2nd ed. San Francisco: Jossey-Bass.

Pascarella, Ernest T., and Charles Blaich. 2013. Lessons from the Wabash National Study of Liberal Arts Education. *Change* 45(2): 6–15.

Patel, E. 2012. *Sacred Ground: Pluralism, Prejudice, and the Promise of America.* Boston: Beacon Press.

Perry, William G., Jr. 1968. *Forms of Intellectual and Ethical Development in the College Years: A Scheme.* New York: Holt, Rinehart, & Winston.

Pizzolato, Jane E. 2005. Creating crossroads for self-authorship: Investigating the provocative moment, *Journal of College Student Development* 46: 624–41.

Pope, Loren. 2000. *Colleges That Change Lives: 40 Schools You Should Know about Even If You're Not a Straight-A Student,* 3rd ed. New York: Penguin Books.

Pope, Loren, and Hilary Massel Oswald. 2012. *Colleges That Change Lives: 40 Schools You Should Know about Even If You're Not a Straight-A Student,* 4rd ed. New York: Penguin Books.

Reed, Sally. 2013. Case studies. In *Ensuring Quality and Taking High-Impact Practices to Scale,* edited by George D. Kuh and Ken O'Donnell, 23–44. Washington, DC: American Association of Colleges and Universities.

Salisbury, Mark H., Brian P. An, and Ernest T. Pascarella. 2013. The effect of study abroad on intercultural competence among undergraduate college students. *Journal of Student Affairs Research and Practice* 50(1): 1–20.

Scott, Sue M. 1997. The grieving soul in the transformation process. In *Transformative Learning in Action: Insights from Practice,* edited by Patricia Cranton, 41–50. San Francisco: Jossey-Bass.

Smith, Barbara L, Jean McGregor, Roberta Matthews, and Faith Gabelnick. 2004. *Learning Communities: Reforming Undergraduate Education.* San Francisco: Jossey-Bass.

Snowden, Dave. 2012. Finding new solutions to wicked problems. Notes from the KM World 2012 Conference, Washington, DC, October 20. http://aboveand beyondkm.com/2012/10/dave-snowdenfinding-new-solutions-to-wicked-prob lemskmworld.html.

Taylor, Edward W. 1998. The theory and practice of transformative learning: A critical review. Information Series No. 374. ERIC Clearinghouse on Adult, Career, and Vocational Education. ERIC number: 423422. Columbus: Ohio State University. http://www.eric.ed.gov/ERICWebPortal/detail?accno=ED423422.

Taylor, Edward W. 2007. An update of transformative learning theory: A critical review of the empirical research (1995–2005). *International Journal of Lifelong Education* 26(2): 173–91.

Taylor, Edward W., and Patricia Cranton. 2012. *The Handbook of Transformative Learning: Theory, Research, and Practice.* San Francisco: Jossey-Bass.

Tinto, Vincent. 2012. *Leaving College: Rethinking the Causes and Cures of Student Attrition.* 2nd ed. Chicago: University of Chicago Press.

Torres, Vasti, Susan R. Jones, and Kristen A. Renn. 2009. Identity development theories in student affairs: Origins, current status, and new approaches. *Journal of College Student Development* 50(6): 577–96.

Wenger, Etienne. 1998. *Communities of Practice: Learning, Meaning and Identity.* New York: Cambridge University Press.

Wesener, Kelly S., Scott Peska, and Monica Trevino. 2010. Healing your community. In *Enough Is Enough: A Student Affairs Perspective on Preparedness and Response to a Campus Shooting,* edited by B. O. Hemphill and B. H. LaBanc, 115–34. Sterling, VA: Stylus.

Winkelmes, Mary-Ann. 2013. Transparency in teaching: Faculty share data and improve students' learning, *Liberal Education*, 99(2). http://www.aacu.org/liberal education/le-sp13/winkelmes.cfm.

Wright, Mary C., Jeffrey L. Bernstein, and Ralph Williams. 2013. The steps of the ladder keep going up. In *Using Reflection and Metacognition to Improve Student Learning*, edited by Matthew Kaplan, Naomi Silver, Danielle LaVaque-Manty, and Deborah Meizlish, 104–21. Sterling, VA: Stylus.

Zachary, Lois J. 2011. *The Mentor's Guide: Facilitating Effective Learning Relationships*. San Francisco: Jossey-Bass.

Zander, Benjamin, and Rosamund S. Zander. 2002. *The Art of Possibility: Transforming Professional and Personal Life*. New York: Penguin Books.